The Secret World of
BATS

JOHN AND MOLLY HINE

Methuen . London

First published in 1986
by Methuen Children's Books Ltd,
11 New Fetter Lane,
London EC4P 4EE.
Text and illustrations © 1986
John and Molly Hines

Printed & bound in Great Britain by
Redwood Burn Limited,
Trowbridge, Wiltshire.

British Library Cataloguing in Publication Data

Hines, John
    The secret world of bats.
    1. Bats—Juvenile literature
    I. Title   II. Hines, Molly
    599.4   QL737.C5
    ISBN 0–416–49030–1
    ISBN 0–416–49040–9 Pbk

DEDICATION

With our grateful thanks to all those kindly householders who, often against their initial instincts, have generously agreed to allow bats to remain as welcome guests in their homes.

ACKNOWLEDGEMENTS

We should like to express our gratitude to Dr. Bob Stebbings of The Institute of Terrestrial Ecology for generously sharing with us, over the years, his knowledge and love of bats. Without his guidance this book could never have been written.

Contents

Illustrations

1 Folklore, fiction and fact

Bats – those little fluttering shadows only half-seen in the twilight – have lived for millions of years in a secret world, a world unknown to anyone but themselves.

Because the lives of bats were surrounded in mystery, it was easy for old folklore and superstition to weave images of bats as the familiars of witches and creatures of the Devil. The tales could never be challenged for nobody knew the truth.

The stories and sayings grew over the years. They ranged from 'They are flying mice!' and 'They get in your hair!' to expressions such as 'Like a bat out of hell' and 'As blind as a bat'. Nobody in the western world had a good word to say for bats. Then, at the end of the 19th. century, a novelist named Bram Stoker wrote a book called 'Dracula'. It was an entertaining horror story and an instant success.

'Dracula' films have done a great deal of harm to the unfortunate bat's image.
(*Scene from 'The Scars of Dracula' – courtesy of The John Kobal Collection*)

A film was made of the book in 1931 and, such was its grip on the imagination, Dracula films have continued to be made ever since.

Unfortunately, Count Dracula was portrayed as an evil half-human creature, capable of turning into a bat and feeding on

human blood. The films succeeded in sharpening all the old fears of bats which people have had over the ages.

Until very recently, bats were treated as vermin. They were killed, often brutally ill-treated and banished from their roosts. Life became increasingly difficult for them for many reasons and their survival was seriously threatened.

In recent years, an increasing number of people have become fascinated by bats, trying to discover the truth and to find out the real nature of their life-style. The fact is that, although we have managed to uncover quite a lot about their lives, a great deal remains undiscovered.

We do know that most of the old folklore is quite untrue. They are not flying mice. In fact, they are not related to rodents in any way. They are more closely related to the Insectivores, which include the hedgehog and mole, and, strange though it may seem, they are related to the Primates, which include man.

Bats are not blind. They can see quite well, although British bats do have rather small eyes.

There is no evidence to support the belief that bats may get in your hair. Bats are extremely skilful flyers and can dodge very small obstacles. Tests have been made with fine wires in the bat's flightpath and they slip through them with ease. We have stood hatless in an attic with several hundred bats flying round us and have never had any problems.

However, baby bats are very inquisitive little creatures and, before they are able to fly, they crawl everywhere, exploring rather like human babies. In our local chapel, baby bats sometimes wander through small knot-holes in the boarded ceiling. When this happens they flutter down helplessly like falling leaves. It is just possible that one could land on someone's head and would naturally clutch on to save itself. Perhaps it was in circumstances like this that the story first started, particularly in the old days before houses had ceilings.

Sometimes it is difficult to convince people that bats are shy, gentle little creatures which ask for nothing more than to be left alone. For example, we are often asked if bats would attack humans. Bats are not aggressive and they would never attack anyone. However, if they are clumsily handled it is only natural that they will be frightened, for they are delicate little animals. They may well try to bite you out of fear, but most British bats have such tiny mouths and weak jaws that they cannot break human skin. However, some of our larger bats are capable of giving a hard nip, but this would only be in an attempt to defend themselves. Even vampire bats are not aggressive, but only bite in order to feed or defend themselves (see page 35).

Bats are very clean animals. They constantly groom themselves and the females also groom their young. They make no nests and so never bring untidy nesting material into their roosts. Whether their roosts are in trees or buildings, bats always enter by existing holes. They never chew woodwork and they have neither the claws nor the strong teeth for making or enlarging holes.

British bats eat only insects and this they do very efficiently. The smallest British bat, the Pipistrelle, can eat over 3,000 insects in a night.

One lady whose colony we survey, has about 300 Pipistrelles in her attic. She rejoices in the fact that they could be eating about a million insects in a night!

Bats like a wide menu and they eat the beneficial insects as well as the pests. However, they do eat those wood-boring insects which are so destructive in buildings and that alone should make them welcome guests.

Because bats' droppings consist only of insect remains, they are dry and not unpleasant. They resemble mouse droppings but, when rubbed in the fingers, they crumble to a fine powder which looks rather like instant coffee. The droppings are very light in weight and an accumulation of many years is said to make an excellent insulation for the attic.

Because bats are not only harmless, but actually beneficial, you would imagine that people would have cared for them and encouraged them. In fact, bats are becoming much less common and, although attitudes are now changing, for some species of bats conservation has come too late.

Bats have few natural enemies. Occasionally owls will kill bats and we have had a number of cases of cats catching bats. The cats usually find the exit from the roost and sit and wait until the bats come out at dusk. Unfortunately, cats can become very skilful bat-catchers once they learn the trick.

It is undoubtedly man who has done the most harm to the innocent bat. Vandals kill them with sticks, airguns and, in one instance of brutality, have actually set fire to sleeping bats! People who have been frightened of them have swatted them like flies. In the past they have been poisoned or smoked out of their roosts. Their exit holes have been blocked up, shutting them out, or even worse, shutting them in to die of starvation.

The destruction of woodland and hedgerows, either for building development or farming, means the loss of roosts and the reduction of insects on which the bats feed. Silage-making on the farms, instead of the old-fashioned hay-making, also cuts down the number of insects which would normally thrive on the flowering hay crop. Farmers use insecticides to control insect pests. This not only kills the insects, but can also kill the bats which feed on poisoned insects.

Certain insects are of special importance to bats. The Cockchafer Beetle, known as the May Bug, is one of these. Its appearance in spring, when the bats are hungry after coming out from hibernation, provides valuable feeding for the Greater Horseshoe Bat. This species is a large bat and needs plenty of food, which could be met by a good supply of the big Cockchafer. Unfortunately, Cockchafers are very destructive of crops and young trees and are considered pests by farmers. Insecticides have almost wiped out this insect and this has probably contributed significantly to the sad decline in the Greater Horseshoe Bat.

Although bats feed on wood-boring insects, bats are usually only in one roost for a few months a year and sometimes only a few days. While they are away, the wood-borers can do some damage. Also, most of the life-cycle of the Common Furniture Beetle, the worst pest, takes place inside the timber and the beetle itself may only make rare and brief appearances.

Although it may take a long time for the damage to be noticed, it is then that the pest control companies are called in. In the past, the favourite chemical used to control wood-worm was Lindane. It is a certain killer of bats and will remain deadly to them for at least 30 years. Happily, there is a new chemical, called Permethrin, which will kill the woodworm, but is harmless to bats. This is the chemical which should always be used when there is any evidence of bats, even if none are present at the time.

The disturbance of bats, particularly during hibernation or breeding can be very damaging. A number of bat species hibernate in the winter in caves, mines and other cave-like places such as disused railway and canal tunnels or old cellars and ice-houses. Caves are, however, fascinating places and the sport of caving is growing rapidly. Although most serious cavers are responsible people and many are conservationists or even bat enthusiasts, any increase in the number of people moving through the bats' roosts can be harmful.

The greatest risk in caves probably comes from the curious visitor rather than the real caver. In their ignorance they may disturb bats without actually wishing them any harm. On one occasion, a cave which was the roost of the rare Greater Horseshoe Bat had been used by children for glue-sniffing parties and a bonfire had been lit in another. In both cases the bats had fled.

Bats and their habitat are in such immediate danger that, unless we act with real determination, many species of bat could vanish within our lifetime.

2 What are bats?

Bats are mammals and, like all mammals, they are warm-blooded and the females suckle their young.

'I don't like bats, because I can't stand anything with feathers!' one old man said to us. On being told that bats don't have feathers, he replied, 'But they fly, don't they?'

He could be forgiven for confusing bats and birds, for the bat is the only mammal which can truly fly. Also, very few people have actually seen a bat close-up, so it is hardly surprising that some imagine that a bat is a kind of bird.

The early ancestors of bats are unknown and we have no way of telling how and when bats first took to the air. However, among the few fossils of early bats which have been discovered is one which is about 50 million years old. The interesting thing about this fossil is that the bat is little different from those of today. This means that bats, in many respects the same as we know them, were among the earliest mammals and were flying millions of years before man first appeared.

Bats have the scientific name of **Chiroptera**, which comes from the Greek and means hand-winged. The world's bats are divided into two groups called **Megachiroptera** and **Microchiroptera**, which simply mean large bats and small bats. All British bats belong to the group of small bats, but the two groups do overlap in size. The most obvious difference is that the Megachiroptera have large eyes and the Microchiroptera have very small eyes.

A close look at a bat's wing clearly shows why it is called hand-winged, for the bat's hand and arm form the main support for the wing.

Apart from their proportions, the bat's hand and arm are remarkably like those of humans in many ways. The bat's upper arm is short and the forearm very long, but it is the thumb and fingers which are so different from the human hand. The thumb is short and has the only claw on the bat's hand. The fingers are delicate and very long and tapered. It is these long fingers which give the wing its correct curved shape for flying.

The membrane which forms the wing is made of two layers of skin. This membrane runs from the shoulders, is stretched over the framework made of the arm and fingers, and then goes down to the legs, ankles and tail.

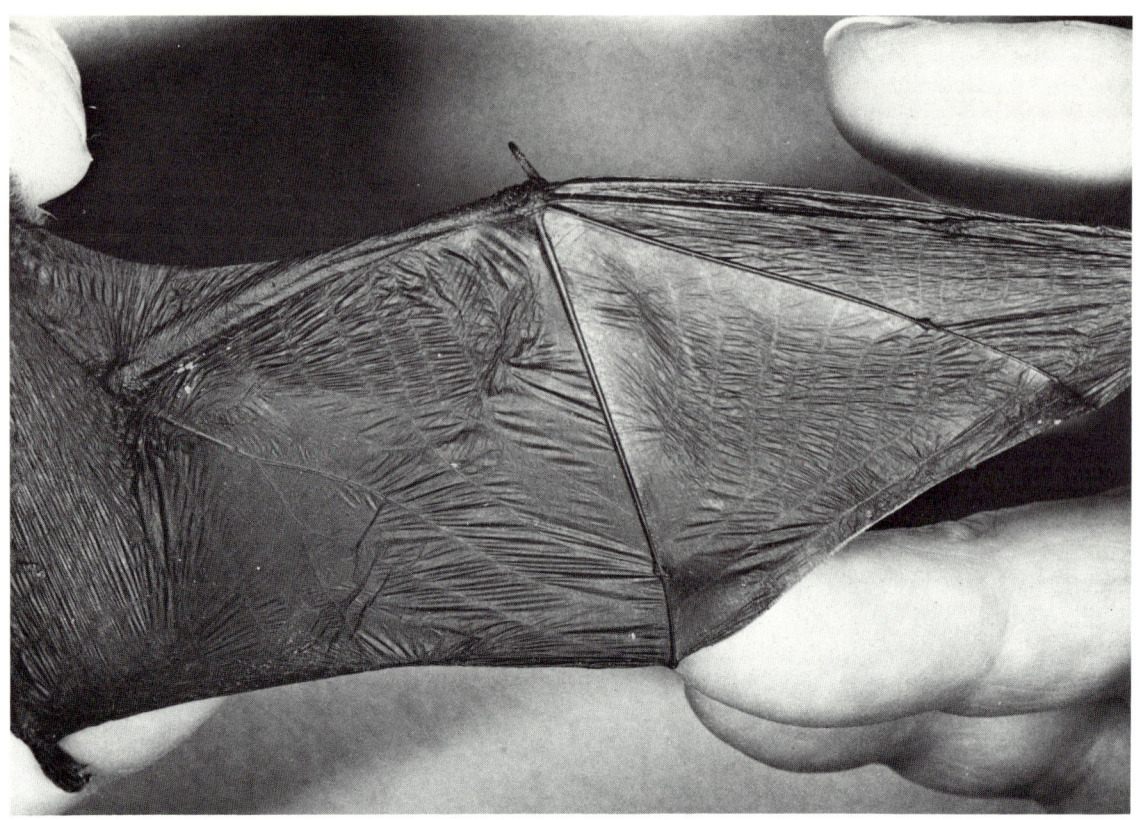

The bat's wing, forearm, fingers and the thumb with its claw.

The membrane is so thin that it is almost transparent when fully stretched, yet it is surprisingly tough. When the wing is at rest, the membrane doesn't hang in folds, but it contracts and thickens like a piece of elastic or stretch tights. Thickening rather than folding is a great benefit, for it helps to retain heat and protects the wing from damage.

The bat's wings are vital for its survival, for it feeds on the wing and a bat which can't fly will starve to death. The membrane has a great number of blood vessels, which provide a good blood supply and helps speedy healing after injuries. Even large holes in the membrane, as large as 20 mm across, will heal rapidly, but if the edge of the membrane is torn, it can be more serious.

Bats have very soft fur, mainly in shades of brown, grey and grey-black. Very young bats usually differ in colour from adults, which helps in identifying the youngsters.

The legs of bats are thin and relatively weak-muscled. Their hip-joints are set at an unusual angle which results in the kneecaps pointing almost backwards. For this reason, their legs hinge in the opposite direction from those of humans. Bats are not well designed for walking, but most species can crawl surprisingly well, taking most of their weight on their front limbs.

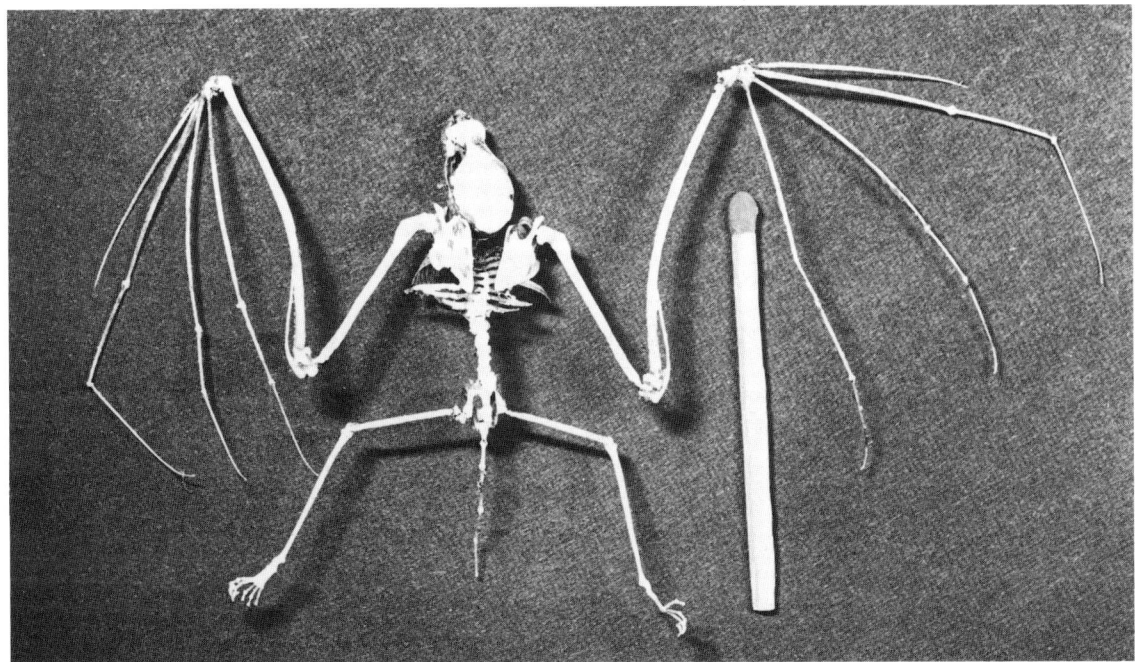

The single claw on their thumbs is used very skilfully, but they are far more expert at holding on with the claws on their toes.

Horseshoe Bats have exceptionally weak legs and have very poor ability for movement on the ground.

Like their kneecaps, bats' feet point roughly backwards. They have five toes on each foot and each toe has a very fine little claw. Holding a bat is a strange experience, for it will immediately cling to the hand so that it feels secure from falling. The delicate claws of the smaller bats will grip with a gossamer-like touch, so light that it can hardly be felt at all. Larger bats, such as the Noctule, can hold on very firmly, but their grip is still not painful.

It is in flight that bats excel, for they are superb on the wing. Because their legs hinge forwards, bats are able to use their legs as well as their arms to beat their wings. This gives them remarkable control in flight, so that some bats can hover, fly sideways and even backwards. They can use the membrane between their legs and tail, called the inter-femoral membrane, as a rudder and also as an air-brake.

Bats may catch insects with their mouths, but often use their wings to scoop them up. If that misses, they have the last chance of using their inter-femoral membrane to catch them. This accounts for some of their apparent tumbling aerobatics when hunting.

Bats belong to a number of species. There are 15 species of

Skeleton of a Lesser Horseshoe Bat. In life the knees would point backwards. The fragility of this bat is clearly seen in comparison with a matchstick.

British bats. These species differ in many ways from each other. Some are so alike that it is difficult to tell them apart, but others vary widely.

Species differ in their flying ability. Some feed by hovering and picking insects off the foliage. Others fly with such accuracy that they can sweep tiny insects from the surface of a pond at speed. Bats with long narrow wings are the ones which can fly fast and those with shorter and wider wings are slower, but more skilful in flight.

Where the membrane joins the ankle and the tail, there is a thin spur of cartilage attached to the ankle and giving strength to the edge of the membrane. This spur is called a calcar. On some bats there is a tiny lobe or flap of membrane standing out from the calcar, called the post-calcarial lobe. It doesn't seem to serve any useful purpose from the bat's point of view, but it is very helpful in one way. Because not all species of bats have this lobe, it can help to identify the species to which a bat belongs.

Identifying our smaller bats can be quite difficult and often a number of points must be checked to make sure. Naturally, the size of a bat is important and the usual way of comparing the size is by measuring the length of the forearm. This is more accurate than trying to measure the wingspan or the length of the body.

Baby bats grow very quickly and, in a few weeks, are about the same size as their mothers. The difference can usually be detected by the colour of their fur and by the joints of their fingers. Baby bats have gently tapered finger joints which are almost transparent when you hold them up to the light. As they get older, you can no longer see through the joints and they become knobbly instead of tapered.

One of the most useful ways of identifying bat species is by their ears, for the ears of bats come in all shapes and sizes, from the small ones of the tiny Pipistrelle to the incredibly large ones of the Long-eared Bat.

Just inside the ears of most British bats is a kind of mini-ear. This is called a tragus. These also are of a variety of shapes and sizes and are a very valuable aid in identification.

Two species of British bats, called the Greater and Lesser Horseshoes, have no tragus, but they do have strange folds of skin around their noses. This is called a nose-leaf. No other British bat has this formation and this makes them very easy to identify.

Other ways of identifying species of British bats include checking their weight, the shape of the male's sexual organs and even the size of their feet!

Of course, the place in which bats are found can be an

important clue to their species. For example, some bats nearly always live in trees and others only winter in caves and similar places. However, bats are intelligent and adaptable and are quick to discover new and more up-to-date roosts, for with the constant loss of roosts they must be adaptable to survive. Several species have found modern centrally-heated houses much to their liking and cavity walls in buildings can be very attractive to them.

Bats can live a surprisingly long time, as much as thirty years. We know this from the ringed animals which are found in their favourite roosts year after year. However, from the same evidence and from the fact that colonies find it so difficult to maintain their numbers, it is obvious that very few bats achieve their full life-span. This is clearly due to the wide range of hazards they face throughout their lives, but we know that many bats die as juveniles.

In some ways bats may appear strange, but they are ideally suited to the life they lead. The bat is such a wonderful little creature that its abilities are almost unbelievable. In fact, when we consider all their skills, bats can truly be called the super-stars of the animal world.

3 Surviving the winter

In warm and tropical countries, bats can find food all the year round, but in colder countries, like Britain, there are few insects about in winter.

Most insect-eating birds migrate for the colder months to tropical or sub-tropical countries where insects are always available. British bats are not long-distance travellers and have to find another way to survive. Their answer is to hibernate.

Many people think that hibernation means finding a warm place to curl up and then merely sleeping the winter away. In fact, it is far more complex. Most animals can't hibernate and, if they tried to, they would die. Clearly, there must be something special about the bat which allows it to survive.

In the autumn, as temperatures get lower and the days get shorter, bats start to eat more and to put on weight. Their weight increases quite rapidly at this time as they store extra fat in their bodies. Then, as the temperature falls even lower and the days get shorter the supply of food dwindles and bats move into their winter hibernation roosts. These may be in caves, buildings, hollow trees or other places, according to the special requirements of the different species.

There are several important points about hibernation roosts. First of all, they must be reasonably safe from disturbance or attack. There must be protection from severe cold and rapid changes of temperature. The roost must be humid, that is, there must be plenty of moisture in the air. Each species has very precise requirements for hibernation roosts and even slight changes in the environment, for example partially closing the entrance to a cave, can force bats to abandon the roost.

The behaviour of bats in their hibernation roosts varies. Some species huddle together for warmth, often with considerable numbers of them in one group. Some roost on their own and others, although they share the same roost and may be close together, never actually touch each other.

Bats in caves use their roosts in a number of ways. Some squeeze themselves into tiny cracks and are almost invisible. Other species hang upside down from the wall or roof of the cave in full view. Strangest of all are the bats which creep in among the stones on the floor of the cave and often burrow quite deeply.

Bats which roost in hollow trees are less protected from severe changes of temperature than bats in caves. For this reason, many tree-hibernating bats like to huddle together for warmth. Such roosts can become extremely cold, dropping below freezing point. In such cases, the bats may have to move. It can obviously be very serious for bats to move when the weather is so cold and the bats may well exchange their tree-roosts for caves or other warmer places.

In winter, cave entrances can be very cold and about the same as the outside temperature. As you go deeper, the temperature rises and changes in temperature are much smaller. Most cave-hibernating bats are found deep in the caves in the really cold weather. They are creatures of habit and, if undisturbed, they will often go back to the same sites year after year.

Once in a suitable roost they become torpid and eventually go into the deep state called hibernation. It is a state requiring important changes in their bodies. The bat's temperature starts to drop. Its breathing gets slower and so does the rate of its heart-beat. Finally, its temperature is usually a little above that of its surroundings. Its breathing and heart-beat are so slow that they are almost imperceptible. In fact, its body mechanism is just 'ticking over' and it is barely alive. In this state it is burning up the smallest amount of fat necessary to keep it just warm enough to survive.

Although they are scarcely alive a computer-like instinct remains on watch. Changes of temperature, intruders coming close to them, supplies of fat getting dangerously low, these and other factors are all registered and the bat can take necessary action.

If danger threatens, a bat in hibernation can't wake up and fly away immediately. First of all it must raise its temperature which, in turn, increases its heart-beat and breathing rates. To start with, it shivers. Shivering, the involuntary contraction of innumerable tiny muscles, is a common way for animals to keep warm. Even humans shiver if they are cold, in an involuntary effort to warm themselves.

The bat's temperature slowly rises, but it could be nearly an hour before it is warm enough to be able to fly. Finally, it becomes active and flies off to a safer place. Unfortunately, it often does this at great cost. In order to raise its temperature, it must burn up precious fat, usually many days' supply. If it is disturbed several times, it may be left with insufficient fat to get through the winter and the bat will starve before the spring arrives. This is one very good reason why hibernating bats should never be disturbed.

If there is a warmer spell during the winter when insects might be about, bats may fly in search of food. This happens particularly if their supply of fat is getting low, in which case their hunting trips are known as starvation-flights. Often this is a desperate gamble to survive as they may burn up a lot of energy in flying and yet find little or no food.

It would be wrong to imagine that bats, if undisturbed, remain unmoving for most of the time. As temperatures change, some bats will move to find the temperature they need, sometimes moving a few feet, sometimes to a different part of a cave or even to a different roost altogether.

A hibernating Greater Horseshoe Bat in a limestone cave in Gwent.

Different species control their hibernation in different ways. Even the sexes behave differently. For example, the female Greater Horseshoe Bat finds a deep part of a cave and moves very little through the winter. The male, however, often keeps nearer the entrance, and moves from time to time. The reason for this is that, before hibernating, the female is usually much fatter than the male and she can afford to find a reasonably cold place and live on her plentiful supply of fat. The male, however, must use his smaller fat supply with greater economy, frequently seeking colder surroundings to lower his metabolism.

Hibernation can be a very difficult time for young bats who will only be a few months old when the need to hibernate arrives. They have had little time to build up their supplies of fat and also they are inexperienced in the skills of winter survival. The fact that they get through the winter at all is a miracle, but, sadly, many young bats do die in their first winter.

We have no precise knowledge of how bats know when it is time to wake up. This is another of the bat's secrets which has still to be solved. Deep in a cave, in complete darkness with no trace of sunlight for months, the bats' instincts tell them that spring has arrived.

Sometimes, of course, spring can be cold, wet and windy, and no insects will be flying. The bats may find that the food, which is now so desperately needed, just isn't about. Poor springs can kill a great number of bats.

Hibernating bats are helpless and vulnerable until they are warm enough to move and escape. They can be attacked by predators, both animal and human. Most common of all is the disturbance by people who don't understand hibernation and probably wish the bats no harm, but are merely curious about them. They find the bats, shine torches on them, even touch them. It is believed that bats can be sensitive to the body heat of a few people standing near to them. This may be enough to raise the temperature of the cave sufficiently for the bat to decide to move.

The fact that a bat remains apparently unconcerned after there has been a disturbance means nothing. The deep state of hibernation may well have been penetrated and the bat may wake up and move later. It is important for everyone to understand that to disturb a hibernating bat, however briefly, may condemn it to death.

4 How bats breed

Some species of the world's bats may have their young at any time of the year, but for British bats the timing of the birth is critical.

The females must be fit and sufficiently well-fed to survive the physical strain of pregnancy and feeding the young. The male also must be active and in good condition for mating. In addition there must be enough time for the young bats to develop and build up their fat reserves for survival through the coming winter.

The problems are complex. Both males and females are usually at their fittest in summer and autumn. However, the female can't become pregnant then, for the young would be born either just before or during winter when the bats should be hibernating. The female would be drained of her strength and reserves and there would be no insects for either mother or young. Clearly, neither would survive.

Bats overcome the difficulties in a way which is unique, for it is unknown in other mammals. British bats mate mainly in autumn at a time when both sexes are fit, although mating does continue into winter.

Both males and females mate a number of times with different partners. The male takes no further interest in either his mate or his offspring. The female doesn't become pregnant at the time of mating, but she stores the sperm within her body and, in some way which we don't fully understand, she nourishes it and keeps it alive. She then hibernates.

In the spring, the female comes out of hibernation and hunts for food. If the feeding is good and she is in reasonable condition, she then produces an ovum. This is fertilised by the stored sperm and she becomes pregnant. If it is a poor spring or if she is unfit, then she may well miss a pregnancy for that year.

In most British bats, the females can breed in their second year, but may not do so until their third or fourth year. The Greater Horseshoe female is very late maturing and usually starts breeding about the fourth year, but it isn't unknown for a female to be as old as ten years before having her first young.

Because female bats have this delay in reaching maturity and only have one baby at a time or even none at all, it is very difficult for a colony to make up any losses or maintain its

Feeding a female Noctule which has just given birth. The baby is under the mother's elbow.

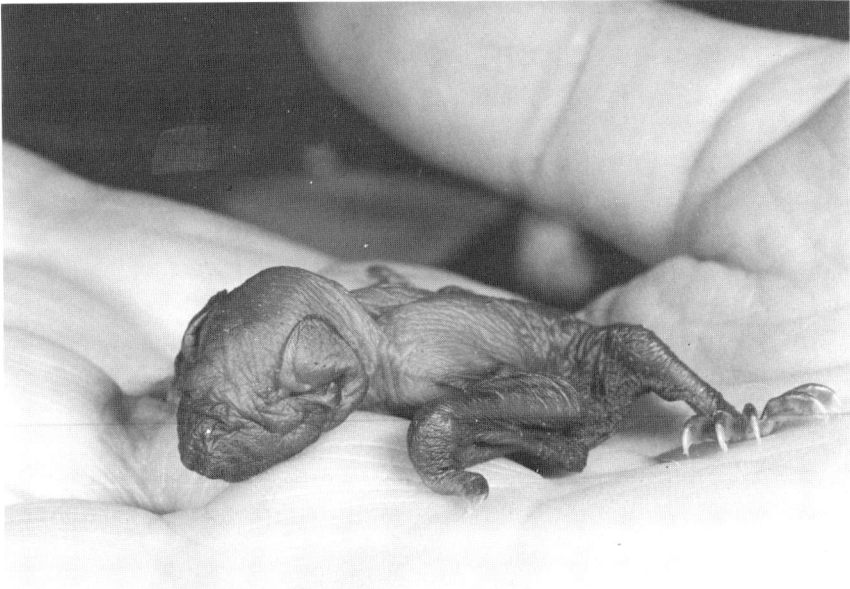

The baby Noctule in the hand at just a few hours old. It is blind and hairless, with its wings undeveloped, but its claws and even tragus are clearly seen.

A Lesser Horseshoe female with a baby about three weeks old. It is already as big as its mother, but the mother is hanging by her feet and the baby is head uppermost.

numbers. For this reason, any natural or man-made disasters may make it impossible for a colony to survive.

The pregnant females start gathering together about mid-May in what is called a breeding or maternity roost. Most species exclude the adult males, but some males are occasionally found in the roost. These roosts are often old-established sites which are particularly suited to the females' needs. They look for warmth and, most important, that they should be safe and free from disturbance. The young are usually born about the end of June and the beginning of July. However, the development of the embryo slows down in poor weather and the exact length of the pregnancy can vary.

Although the maternity roosts may have been used for many years, sometimes the bats miss a year, or they may arrive, stay a few days and then leave, not returning until the next year. The reason for this behaviour is unknown, but disturbance or extremes of weather may often be the cause.

At the moment of birth, the females generally turn head uppermost and the baby drops into the pouch formed by the interfemoral membrane joining the legs and tail. The female wraps her wings round her baby and suckles it. Although the mother has two teats, twins are rare in British bats.

Female Horseshoe bats have, in addition, two 'false teats'. These are low down on her abdomen and produce no milk. The babies can use these as 'dummies'. They can also hang on to them, if it is necessary for the mother to fly with them.

Even after they have given birth, the mothers can still leave the roost and move elsewhere if they are seriously disturbed. It is on these occasions that they will carry their babies with them, the youngsters hanging tightly to their mothers' fur. For this reason, it is most important that breeding roosts should not be disturbed and naturalists rarely enter them while the females are present.

If there are few insects about and feeding is very poor, females may abandon their young. Their instinct tells them that it is far better for the colony if the females survive to breed another year, rather than both mothers and young dying of starvation.

Although young bats can fly at about three weeks old, they climb about with great agility before this. Unfortunately, this sometimes results in their falling out of roosts and being separated from their mothers. If a young bat is found crawling on the ground, it should be picked up very gently and put in a ventilated box until just before dusk. It should then be put outside, as close to the entrance to the roost as possible. It is important that it should be out of the way of cats.

When the adult bats come out, the baby will cry to its mother

with what are known as 'isolation cries'. The mother will probably
come down and rescue it. If, however, the baby isn't rescued,
then it will have to be cared for. This is explained later (see page
46).

When babies are flying, the mothers continue to feed them for
about another two weeks, after which they are normally self-
sufficient.

Shortly after weaning, the females leave the roost. It isn't long
before the young follow and, about the end of August, the
breeding roost is usually empty until the next year.

Some species of bats may be found in small numbers in
breeding roosts at other times of the year. In some of our Lesser
Horseshoe breeding roosts, for example, we often find bats, even
in January if the weather is mild. Then, if the weather turns
frosty, they disappear to their hibernation sites again.

Very little is known about the movements of bats between their
breeding and hibernation sites. Despite marking bats with
numbered rings and even attaching tiny radio-transmitters to
them, they nearly all seem to disappear. We presume that they
have moved to roosts which are close to good feeding grounds,
in order to build up their reserves for winter. Unfortunately, their
precise movements are another secret which we have yet to
discover.

Females gather in breeding roosts from a wide area. For some
species, they may have come from several hundred square miles.
It is easy to see how vital these roosts are and how the loss of a
breeding roost could be disastrous to the bat population of a local
species.

5 'Seeing' in the dark!

Bats can fly and hunt in the dusk or even in the darkness of a moonless night. They fly in cave and mine systems, deep under the earth's surface, through narrow openings, dodging obstacles, weaving round intricate twists and turns of passages, all at high speed and with apparent ease. They never seem to brush their surroundings or each other.

Since ancient times, bats were believed to have the ability of seeing in the dark. It was a skill which defied explanation and so people suspected the supernatural. They reasoned that, if a creature could see in total darkness, then it could only do so with assistance from the Devil.

An 18th-century Italian scientist, named Spallanzani, became intrigued by the bat's ability to navigate in the dark and conducted a series of experiments. He even blinded bats in an attempt to discover their secret.

Spallanzani was nearly successful, for he found that blind bats could still fly and hunt successfully. He then sealed up their ears and discovered that this made bats quite helpless at night flying. However, he was unable to interpret his results and could find no answer to how bats could possibly 'see' with their ears.

Obviously, if bats hunt in total darkness, they need some extraordinary skill in order to survive. Fortunately, they have it. It is called ultra-sound navigation or echo-location.

Man has known a little about echo-location for a long time. In the days of sail, one of the great dangers was navigating in iceberg latitudes in poor visibility. Sailors found that, by using a whistle, they could often hear a warning echo come back from a nearby iceberg.

Blind people can sometimes develop the knack of hearing an echo of the tapping of their stick to warn them of obstacles in their path. Now an aid for the blind, called a sonic torch, has been developed, using this principle.

A form of echo-location was developed during the First World War for detecting submarines. The system was also used for measuring the depths of oceans and to enable fishing fleets to detect shoals of fish. The principle is that pulses of sound are beamed towards a target and the returning echo is picked up by sensitive receivers. The distance of the target is calculated from the time it takes for the echo to return.

Radar, the detecting system using radio-waves, works on a similar principle.

Although there is much to be discovered of how a bat uses ultra-sound, we do know that echo-locating bats have been using the system for millions of years. Their equipment is incredibly small and its effectiveness is superb.

Bats' echo-location uses tiny pulses of sound which they make through their mouths or noses. Some species use both. The echo rebounds from the object, the bat hears it and instantly translates it into an impression in its mind. By moving its head and sending out whole beams of pulses, the bat builds up an almost instant picture of its surroundings. As it flies, the picture is constantly changing, but the bat is aware of even minute obstacles in its path and dodges them with ease.

Even more remarkable is the way bats use their echo-location skills to catch tiny insects for food. The stream of pulses bounces back from the insect which may also be moving. The bat instantly 'sees' the insect's speed and direction and homes in on it with deadly accuracy. As it gets closer to the insect, the number of pulses in a second increases, giving the bat an accurate location on its prey.

Many people think a bat flies haphazardly, rather like a butterfly, but this is not true. The bat's strange zig-zag flight is unpredictable to us but very purposeful for them, as they fly rapidly from insect to insect in a constant search for food.

The bat may have superb echo-location but it doesn't have things all its own way. Quite a number of insects can detect ultra-sound and have methods of trying to dodge the bat's attack. Some wait until the bat is almost upon them and then fold their wings and drop like a stone. Others, such as the Tiger Moths, can emit their own ultra-sound, which may confuse the bat and allow the insect to escape. It is also believed that some insects' ultra-sound may be a warning that the insect has an unpleasant taste.

The frequencies used by bats are very high. Some of the lowest ones can be heard by young children, but, as we grow older, our ability to hear the higher frequencies fades. Many bats use frequencies which are far above the range of the most sensitive human ear. The highest frequency used by a British bat is about 120 kHz, which is that of the Lesser Horseshoe Bat, and is about six times higher than the human ear's range.

Naturalists find it very helpful to be able to listen in to the ultrasounds of bats. Instruments are now available to pick up the bats' cries and translate them to a lower frequency which is within the human range. Such an instrument is called a Bat Detector and the simplest model looks rather like a small transistor radio.

The Bat Detector has a tuning dial and can be set to a wide range of frequencies. The microphone is pointed in the direction of the bat and the tuning dial set to a likely frequency. If nothing is heard, the tuning can be altered until the bat's sounds are picked up. They are heard as a variety of clicks or twitters.

Electronic Bat-detector which can be tuned to pick up the bat's high-frequency navigation sounds.

Certain British bats use frequencies and other characteristics that are distinctive for their species and this is invaluable in helping to identify bats in flight. Some species emit sounds that resemble those of other species and this makes it more difficult. However, experienced naturalists can become very skilful with a detector by noting, not only the frequency, but also the type of sound that is heard.

Some bats are more difficult to pick up on detectors except at close range. This is because their pulses of ultra-sound are very soft and, for this reason, these species are sometimes known as 'whispering' bats.

The Long-eared Bat is one of these species and, as most of its feeding is done by hovering and picking its food off foliage, loud, long-range pulses would be unnecessary. In fact, the soft transmissions are probably an advantage, for they are less likely to warn those insects which can detect ultra-sound.

Bats do make other sounds. For example, they use lower frequencies for communicating with each other. This is often audible just before sunset when the bats are waking up ready for their feeding flights. The sound of their excited twittering may be heard coming from the roost from some distance away.

When a whole colony of bats is flying, there must be a tremendous volume of ultra-sound, particularly in a cave or an attic. Bats must be able to tell their own pulses from those of their neighbours, but we have no idea how they do it.

As each pulse of sound is very loud, one would imagine that bats would tend to deafen themselves and the continuous stream of shrill cries would make it impossible for them to hear the echoes. Fortunately, one of the bat's amazing secrets has been discovered. As it makes each cry, certain muscles in its ears contract and deaden the sound for a moment. This is sufficient to prevent the bat deafening itself, but the muscles relax again in time to hear echoes a split second later.

Bats are experts at echo-location, but they can make occasional mistakes. Often it is due to carelessness. It has been noticed that bats tend to follow the same route over their feeding ground and it is when they are really familiar with it that they may make mistakes. Naturalists use a number of techniques to catch bats and often rely on the bat's errors to do so. However, the bat learns very quickly and it would be very difficult to catch it out twice in quick succession.

Despite our Bat Detectors and electronic equipment, some details of the bat's skills in ultra-sound navigation are a mystery to us and probably will always remain so. It is impossible for humans to imagine the real nature of the ultra-sound picture which is 'seen' by the bat.

Some species of bats nod their heads as they fly and some wag their ears. We are sure this is associated with their navigation, but precisely how is unknown.

The tragus, that mini-ear which is inside the main ear of all but two species of British bats, is believed to play a part in echo-location, but we can only guess at its function.

The two species without a tragus, the Greater and Lesser Horseshoe Bats, have nose-leaves. Again, although we know a little about the nose-leaf, its full purpose is a mystery. It certainly doesn't replace the tragus, for some bats in other parts of the world have both tragus and nose-leaf. The horseshoe-shaped part of the nose-leaf is probably used like a megaphone to give directional control over the pulses of ultra-sound which Horseshoe bats emit from their noses.

Other animals use ultra-sound. Perhaps it is hardly surprising that shrews and hedgehogs use it, for they are Insectivores and are related to bats. However, there can be few creatures, if any, with such a sophisticated echo-location system as the bat.

Finally, the bat's eyesight must be mentioned for it can play its part in the bat's feeding ability. Some bats feed on the ground and from foliage and the eyes are probably used in these cases. Bats in captivity will eat readily from food offered in the fingers and there is no doubt that they are quite sharp-eyed in this respect.

We have to admit that our knowledge of how bats echo-locate is very limited and we have discovered only a little since the early experiments of Spallanzani. In the field of ultra-sound navigation alone, the bat has innumerable secrets which man is never likely to share.

6 Bats in Britain

There are over 900 species of bats in the world, but only fifteen species are recognised as resident in Britain. Several of these are now rare and one species is on the verge of disappearing.

Some species of British bats can be very difficult to identify. The best way to do so is by handling bats under the guidance of an expert, but for handling otherwise a licence is required.

In this chapter it is not our intention to give a key for identification, but only a broad idea of British species and some ways in which they differ.

There are two families of British bats – the Vespertilionids and the Rhinolophids, with thirteen species in the Vespertilionid family and two in the Rhinolophid family. The more common British bats are all Vespertilionids.

The Pipistrelle, *Pipistrellus pipistrellus.* This is the most common British bat. It is the one most usually found in houses and is also our smallest bat, weighing, on average, 5 or 6 grams.

The Pipistrelle is our most common bat and the one most frequently found in houses. It is fairly easily identified by its small size, stubby tragus and post-calcarial lobe.

Pipistrelles are usually found in attics, under roofing felt, behind hanging tiles or in any protected small opening in the roof. Because they like squeezing into restricted spaces, they are among those bats sometimes known as 'crevice creepers'.

Female breeding colonies may be very large, often of several hundred bats. Despite their relatively large numbers, we know little about the Pipistrelle's movements in spring, autumn and winter, for most of these large colonies just seem to disappear.

The Pipistrelle is easily tamed and we have kept an injured male in captivity for nearly two years.

A Brown Long-eared Bat. Its ears can be erected for flight or folded at rest. The long ears give it an attractive appearance.

The Common or Brown Long-eared Bat, *Plecotus auritus.*
This is probably the second most common bat. Originally a forest bat, it has readily adapted to houses and breeding colonies are frequently found in attics.

It is easily identified by its huge, hare-like ears. It could only be confused with its rare relative the Grey Long-eared *Plecotus austriacus*, but, as this is so scarce, a mistake is unlikely.

Those large ears are quite vulnerable and the bat curls them up at rest. When sleeping or hibernating, their ears are tucked away under their arms, just leaving the tragus protruding. Apart from being safer, this also helps to conserve heat.

Brown Long-eared Bats feed mainly by hovering and picking insects off foliage, although they do also feed on the wing. It is one of the 'Whispering bats', giving soft echo-locating pulses which are difficult to pick up on the Bat Detector unless close at hand. It is easily tamed.

A Long-eared Bat at rest with one ear partially curled and the other safely tucked under its arm. Note the tragus remains projecting.

Daubenton's Bat, *Myotis daubentoni.* This is often known as the Water Bat because of its habit of skimming the surface of ponds and streams in search of insects. Although other bats have the same habit, none hunts the water so persistently.

It is mainly recognised by its very large feet, together with the shape and size of its ears and tragus.

Daubenton's Bat is widespread and fairly common. It roosts in buildings, hollow trees and tunnels, particularly canal tunnels. In winter it is found in caves, mines and similar places, where it often crawls into tiny cracks and is practically invisible. It also has the unusual habit of burrowing into the scree and debris on the cave floor, sometimes being found at a considerable depth.

The Whiskered Bat, *Myotis mystacinus.* This bat is fairly widespread, but is more common in south of Britain. It is a handsome animal, rather like Daubenton's Bat, but has smaller feet and a pointed tragus. Its fur is grey and grey-black.

Large colonies may be found in buildings, but little is known of its hibernation habits.

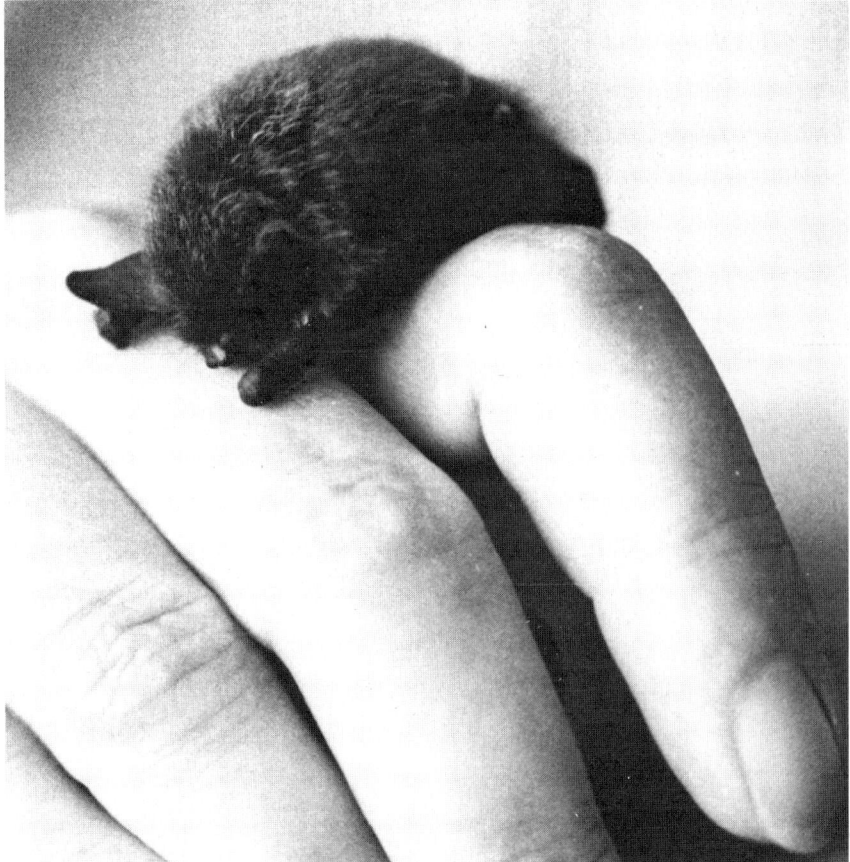

A baby Whiskered Bat, not yet able to fly, asleep on the back of Molly's hand.

Brandt's Bat, *Myotis brandti.* This bat is very similar to the Whiskered Bat, from which it can only be distinguished with great difficulty. In fact, it is only in fairly recent years that they were recognised as separate species.

The Mouse-eared Bat, *Myotis myotis.* The Mouse-eared Bat is very large. It is extremely rare and unlikely to be seen.

This species has never been common in Britain and the last known colony was in Sussex. Unfortunately, the location of the breeding roost was unknown. In 1974, all the females left their hibernating roost for the breeding roost and none returned. What disaster overcame them has never been discovered.

The males of the species continued to gather each year looking for a mate, but no females arrived. The males have disappeared one by one and last year a solitary middle-aged male arrived as the sole known survivor of this species in Britain. By the time this book is published the Mouse-eared Bat may have disappeared from Britain possibly for ever.

Natterer's Bat, *Myotis nattereri*. This is a medium sized bat which is fairly widespread. It roosts in trees and houses and is also found in caves. It is distinguished by having a row of short stiff hairs along the edge of part of the interfemoral membrane.

Bechstein's Bat, *Myotis bechsteini*. This is a very rare bat. However, that has not always been the case. During the excavation of Stone Age flint mines in Norfolk, a great number of bats' bones were found. A high proportion of these were of Bechstein's Bats. It is very similar to Natterer's Bat, but has no row of hairs on the tail membrane.

The Noctule, *Nyctalus noctula*. The Noctule is one of our largest bats. It lives almost entirely in trees and is rarely found in

The Noctule is one of our largest bats. It is very much a woodland bat and depends on old trees.

buildings. They are often found in abandoned woodpecker holes. They prefer to roost high up in the tree, usually at least 5 metres above the ground. They tend to fly and feed much higher than most bats.

In very cold weather, the temperature in trees may fall to a dangerous level and Noctules may be forced to leave the trees and resort to caves and similar places.

Because of the Noctules' dependence on trees, the practice of felling old trees as soon as they start to decay is very serious for this species. It is not always because people don't care, but because they are unaware of the bats' presence and many Noctules are accidentally injured or killed during tree felling.

We know little of the Noctule's habits, because its roosts are rarely seen. It may well be more plentiful than we believe.

It is easily identified by its large size, its broad, rounded tragus and its post-calcarial lobe. It could be confused with Leisler's Bat, *Nyctalus leisleri*, but the Noctule is generally larger.

Leisler's Bat is relatively rare. There had been few records of this species being seen in Britain until recently. Now more are being identified, but nobody is sure whether this means an increase in their numbers or whether it is due to a greater enthusiasm for bats and more people looking for them.

The Serotine, *Eptesicus serotinus*. The Serotine has been mainly found in the south of England and East Anglia, but appears to be working its way north. It has been described as our most building dependent bat.

The Barbastelle, *Barbastella barbastellus*. The Barbastelle is hardly ever seen and has always been considered rare. Yet, a naturalist friend of ours found one last year, sharing a roost with Lesser Horseshoe Bats.

It is very easily identified by its flat, almost pug-face and its broad ears which meet between its eyes. It may be found in trees, buildings and caves.

The Greater Horseshoe Bat, *Rhinolophus ferrumequinum*. The Greater Horseshoe Bat has been vanishing fast over the last

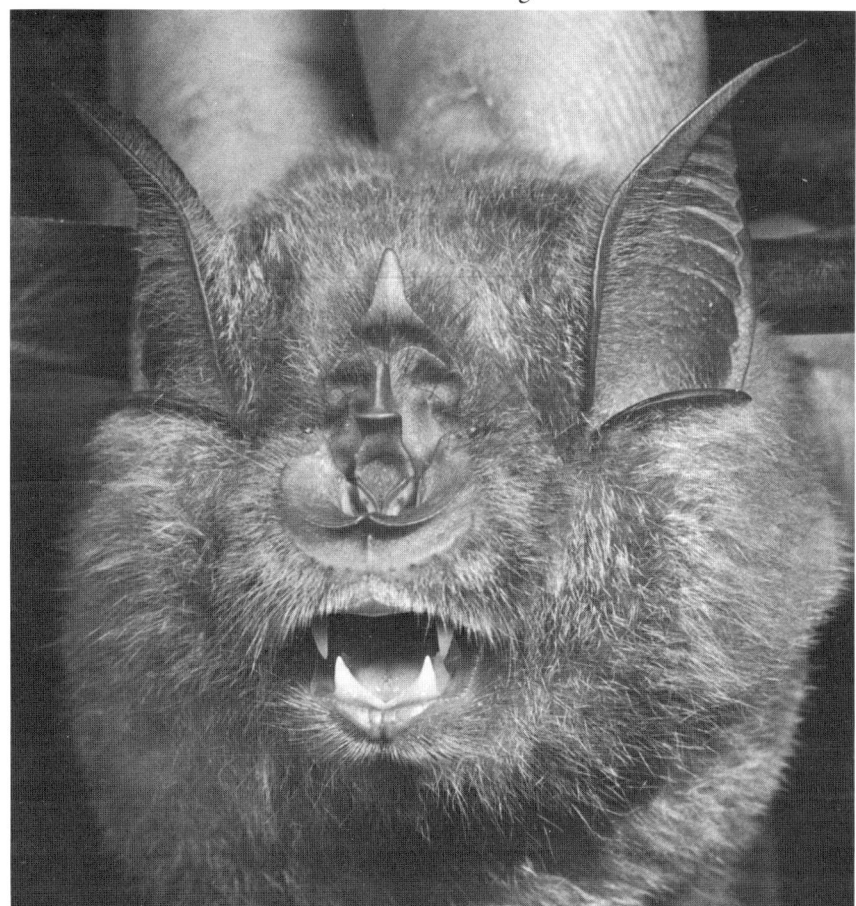

This Greater Horseshoe is looking rather fearsome, but this is only a display because she is afraid.

century. Previously it was widely found in the south of England, but is now confined to south Wales and south-west England. It is estimated that there are only about 2,500 of these bats left.

It is a large bat and is easily identified by the pronounced nose-leaf on its face. This is made up of three parts, but the most obvious is the pronounced horseshoe-shaped skin formation which surrounds its nose and from which it gets its name. The only other bat in Britain with a nose-leaf is the Lesser Horseshoe, but the considerable difference in size easily distinguishes them.

The Greater Horseshoe is very dependent on caves and cave-like places, such as tunnels, mines and derelict cellars, for its hibernation. They are creatures of habit and are found regularly in the same hibernation sites. Their breeding roosts are normally in buildings, usually deserted and free from disturbance.

When occupying caves they tend to gather together, but don't huddle. They hang separately from the roof, looking rather like medium-sized pears. They completely enclose themselves in their wings, which gives them protection from dripping water and helps to keep them warm.

Unlike other British bats, the Horseshoes only emit their echo-locating pulses through their noses. They use their horseshoe-shaped nose-leaf as a sort of megaphone to direct the sound. They use very high frequencies which can easily be identified with a Bat Detector.

The females don't normally breed until they are three or four years old and some are very much older before having their first young. This makes it particularly difficult for this species to make good any losses it may suffer due to bad weather, disturbance or vandalism.

It relies very heavily on the large Cockchafer Beetle for its spring feeding and the scarcity of this beetle has probably contributed to the decline of the Greater Horseshoe. Later in the season it eats the Dor Beetle and the Dung Beetle.

Dr. Roger Ransome has made a lifetime study of this species and we are indebted to him for much of our current knowledge. Together with Dr. Bob Stebbings, of the Institute of Terrestrial Ecology, they have been responsible for the construction of grills at the entrances of caves and mines in order to protect valuable roosts from unauthorised disturbance. This is vitally important work and is widely supported by the Nature Conservancy Council, the World Wildlife Fund, the Mammal Society and other conservation charities and organisations.

The Lesser Horseshoe Bat, *Rhinolophus hipposideros.* The

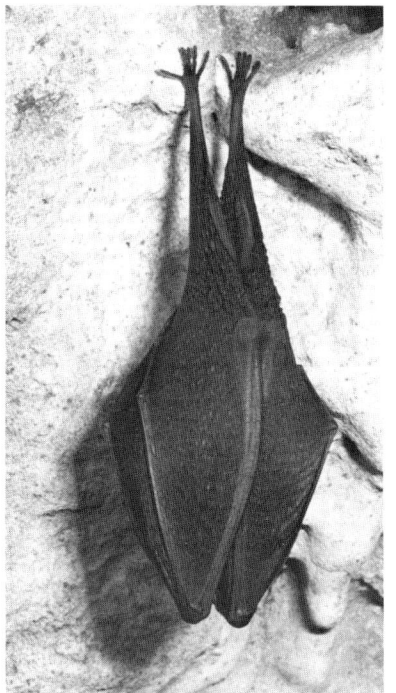

Lesser Horseshoe is, in most respects, a miniature of the Greater Horseshoe. Its habits are mainly the same. Although numbers are diminishing, they are more common than the Greater Horseshoe. It is subject to the same problems of disturbance in caves.

The Greater Horseshoe is very difficult to keep in captivity, but the Lesser Horseshoe is probably the most delicate of all British bats. In captivity it dies within a few days. It is very sensitive to disturbance and is, in every way, a very vulnerable little bat.

The Lesser Horseshoe isn't dependent on the large beetles eaten by the Greater Horseshoe for they would be far too large for it. This does give them a better choice of feeding.

A Lesser Horseshoe Bat hibernating in an ancient iron-mine in Gwent. The bat's tendons are arranged so that their feet continue to grip during deep-hibernation and even death.

Lesser Horseshoes in a Gwent roost.

Britain has less than 2% of the world's bat species. For all practical purposes, the Mouse-eared Bat has gone and many other species are severely endangered. It is quite feasible that Britain will have no bats in a few decades unless public attitudes change and practical conservation becomes more dynamic.

7 Bats round the world

The many bat species in the world form about a quarter of all the existing mammal species put together. They vary greatly in appearance and life-style and the only factor which they seem to have in common is that, almost without exception, their survival is seriously threatened.

We have selected a small number of those species which are sufficiently important or are particularly fascinating in order to give some insight into the complexity of the world's bats.

About three-quarters of all bat species live on insects. The majority of the remaining species are fruit-eating, which makes Fruit Bats, or Flying Foxes as they are sometimes called, very important. They are the only family belonging to the Megachiroptera group. It is a large family with many species, ranging from the world's largest bat, with a wing-span of nearly 2 metres, to tiny bats even smaller than many Microchiroptera.

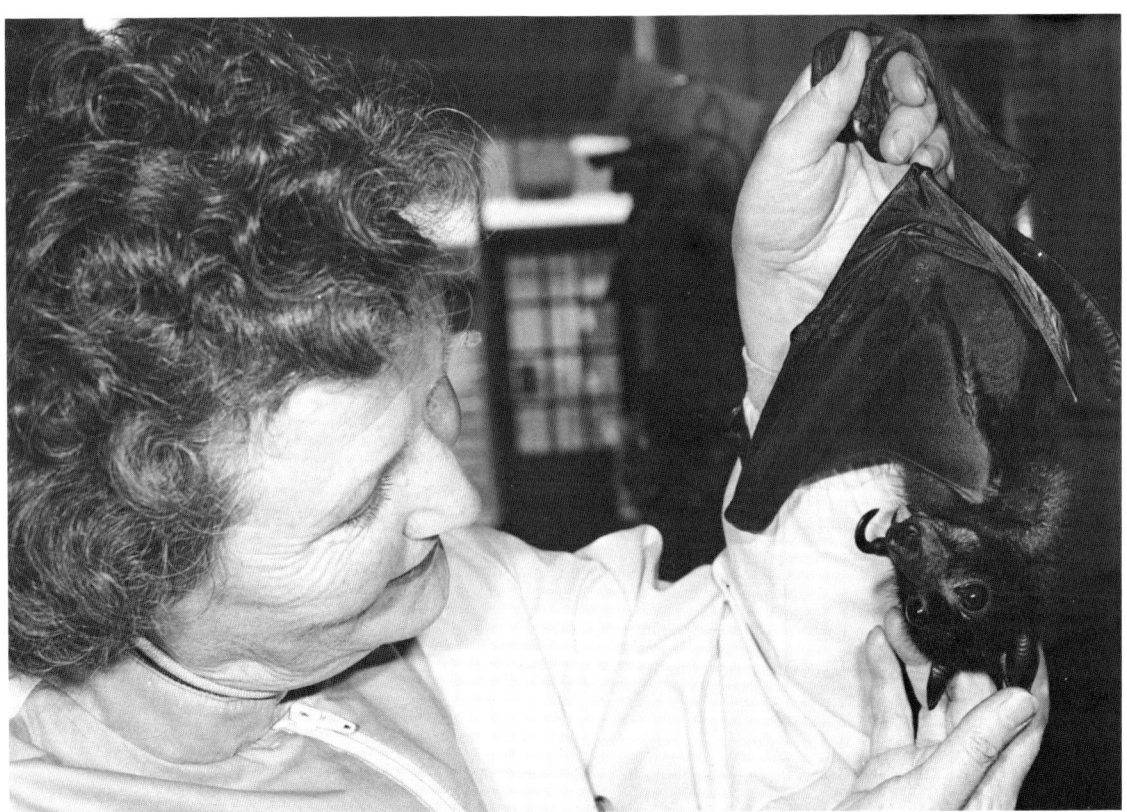

Molly holding a fruit bat.

Hardly any of the Fruit Bat species use echo-location. In fact, they don't need it, for nearly all of them live in the open, not in caves, and they don't hunt moving prey. In contrast to the Microchiroptera, they have large eyes, giving them excellent eye-sight in poor light. Unlike most other bats, Fruit Bats have a keen sense of smell which enables them to detect ripe fruit with ease.

Fruit Bats are considered pests by fruit farmers in many parts of the world, particularly in Australia. However, they do have an important use, because they spread the fruit-seed in their droppings, which helps the survival of some wild species of trees.

Fruit Bats often sleep in trees, hanging quite openly like the fruit they feed on. Others tuck themselves away among the foliage and keep out of sight. Our son told us of Fruit Bats using the furled sails of his cruiser for overnight roosts off Malaysia. They came tumbling out when the sails were unfurled in the morning!

Most bats in this family look fairly similar and are rather dog-like in appearance, but there are some strange exceptions. The most odd-looking must be the Hammer-headed Bat from Africa, whose face resembles that of a horse. It has a deep baritone voice, which is unique in the bat world.

The most famous of all bats is probably the Vampire. It is responsible for a great deal of the misconceptions in people's minds and its Dracula-image has become associated with most bats. Although the true facts have been confused by fiction, the Vampire does drink blood and is a pest which preys on livestock in Central and South America.

The Common Vampire is quite small. It has a strange little face and almost looks as if it has a smirking grin. With its long legs, it is very agile on the ground. It lands near its prey and creeps cautiously up to it. It can actually jump, which enables it to leap out of the way if its quarry wakes up and moves suddenly.

Contrary to popular belief, it does not use fangs, but sharp-edged front teeth. With these it takes a delicate slice off the skin. It then laps the blood with its tongue. Its saliva has three ingredients which prevents the blood from clotting. This is a further disadvantage to its victim, which can go on bleeding after the Vampire has left.

The Vampire can drain a great deal of blood from domestic animals by going back night after night and the smaller victims can actually die eventually from loss of blood.

Vampires can feed on human beings, but rarely do so. Opportunities are few and people are more wary than animals, so domestic animals are the easier and more usual prey.

Vampires spread diseases through their bite, the most serious of which is rabies. This fact makes the Vampire the only bat species which is really harmful to man and his livestock.

Various methods have been used to control the Vampires. One of the most successful has been to net the bats and spread their fur with a highly poisonous paste. When the Vampires return to their roost, they all groom each other, quickly spreading the poison through the whole colony.

Rabies can be carried by any mammal, including dogs and cats. Fortunately, thanks to strict quarantine controls, there is no rabies in Britain.

The Guano Bats get their name from the vast deposits of droppings which have built up in the roosts of some long-established colonies. The guano is highly nitrogenous and makes very rich and valuable agricultural fertiliser. It is so high in nitrogen that, in the past, it has even been used in the manufacture of explosives. Some guano deposits have probably been accumulating for tens of thousands of years and, in some places, are as much as 15 metres deep.

Large Guano Bat colonies roost in the cave systems of Texas and New Mexico. In some of the caves their numbers have been estimated at several million, but even these are seriously declining. The most famous colony is in the Carlsbad Caverns of New Mexico, where the sight of clouds of bats emerging in the evening has become a popular attraction for tourists. The Caverns are now protected as a National Park.

Kitti's Hog-nosed Bat is believed to be the smallest bat in the world. Because of its small size, it is also known as the Bumblebee Bat. Only recently discovered, it is a cave-dweller in Thailand where it has a degree of protection. It has been nominated by the International Union for Nature as one of the most endangered animals in the world.

Centurio senex comes from South America. It is known as 'The Old Man of a Hundred', because of its wrinkled hairless face. The loose folds of skin around its chin give it a very odd appearance. However, even more strange is the fact that it can pull these folds of skin up over its face when it wishes to sleep. Stranger still are the translucent panels in the skin which correspond with the bat's eyes and can be used like windows for the bat to keep watch through. As if that were not enough, the bat also wraps its wings round its face and these too have 'windows'!

The Naked Bat, which comes from South-east Asia, is one of the largest insectivorous bats in the world. As its name implies, it is practically hairless. It has very long pointed wings which would be a great nuisance when resting. This is overcome by the bat having pouches into which the wings neatly fold. Unfortunately, there is no way in which the bat can clean these pouches and, after a time, they would become a bit smelly and unhygienic. Happily, nature seems to have provided the answer in the shape of a species of large earwig which lives in the pouches and keeps them clean. It isn't a parasite and does the bat no harm.

There are only two species of bats in New Zealand, the Long-tailed Bat and the Short-tailed Bat, but they are particularly interesting. They were the only mammals found naturally on the islands, all the others on there were introduced by man. They have never been common in living memory, but they are now very rarely seen and are threatened with extinction.

Little is known of the habits, the needs or the reasons for the decline of these two species. Without such information, conservation measures are virtually impossible. Fossils have been found which show that other bat species have existed in New Zealand in the past, but are now extinct. Sadly, the Long-tailed and Short-tailed Bats seemed doomed to follow.

The Nectar-eating and Pollen-eating Bats are very valuable for they pollinate a great number of trees and shrubs which are of economic importance. Many fruits are dependent on bat-pollination and could well disappear without their aid. The prickly Durian fruit, much loved by the Chinese and Malaysian people, is almost entirely pollinated by one species of bat which is now seriously declining.

Fisherman Bats are found in Central and South America. They are extremely skilful at detecting fish near the surface of the water. They swoop down and grip the fish in their huge sharp claws and fly to a roost to eat them.

There have been reports of Daubenton's Bat, the British Water Bat, catching fish but this has never been confirmed.

In addition to those few we have mentioned, fascinating bats occur in almost endless variety throughout the world and there is the real possibility that others have still to be discovered. Yet, such is the threat to bats, they could disappear before we ever know of their existence.

These threats to bats are worldwide, but the nature of the threats varies from country to country. The people of the Far East don't share the Western fear and dislike of bats. They see bats as creatures of good not evil. Stylised representations of bats are widely used in many Chinese art forms and are said to represent the blessings of health, long-life, virtue, prosperity and natural death. The result is that bats are not persecuted from fear, but they are still in need of conservation.

In the Far East, Africa and even Australia, bats are considered a delicacy and eating them is becoming increasingly popular. In

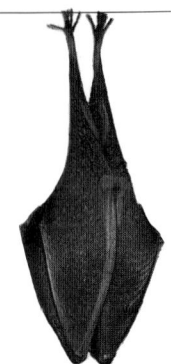

many cases, they are simply caught in vast numbers by placing a net across the entrance to their cave, providing an easy and rich harvest for this profitable market. The result has been an inevitable sharp decline in these species and, unless positive steps are taken for their conservation, their extinction cannot be far away.

In some parts of the world, bats are the ingredients in bizarre folk medicine and witchcraft. The result is undoubtedly ineffective for the user and disastrous for the bats.

In the Netherlands, limestone tunnels which are the breeding and hibernating sites for several thousands of bats have been systematically destroyed in order to provide limestone for the cement industry.

The story can be repeated in innumerable ways across the world. Bat Conservation International, a group of The Fauna and Flora Preservation Society, is making every effort to establish co-ordinated world-wide conservation of bats, but again we must ask the question, 'For many species of bats, aren't we too late?'

8 Bats and the law

Bats throughout the world have had little protection from the law. In many countries where there is some protection, it is rarely enforced.

In 1975, Britain gave the Greater Horseshoe and Mouse-eared Bats special protection, because both species were in danger of disappearing. Unfortunately, it came too late for the Mouse-eared Bat and the Greater Horseshoe's survival is balanced on a knife-edge.

The Wildlife and Countryside Act, 1981, gave far-reaching protection to all species of British bats. As with so many of our wild creatures and plants, protection only seems to be provided when their survival is at such high risk that it is almost impossible to reverse the trend. This is not the fault of the conservation groups, but of the tardiness of the legislators.

The new Act makes it illegal for any unlicensed person to intentionally kill, injure or even handle a wild bat. It is against the law to possess a bat, dead or alive, and bats must not be disturbed at their roosts. However, a sick or injured bat can be cared for and a bat which is so severely injured that it could not recover can be painlessly destroyed. Obviously, anyone finding a sick or injured bat, should seek the guidance of the Nature Conservancy Council or a licensed batworker.

It is illegal to photograph bats unless licensed to do so, except when they are flying freely in the open. Even our own quite comprehensive licences only permit us to photograph bats as incidental to our conservation work. As in all activities with protected species, the welfare of the animal must always come first.

The protection of bats' roosts is vitally important. They must not be destroyed or damaged, nor must access be obstructed to any place which a bat uses for shelter, even if the bats are not present at the time. This applies to dwelling-houses, with the exception that bats may be gently removed from the living quarters of a house, but not from the attic. In all other cases, bats must not be disturbed without consultation with the NCC.

Should it be necessary to work in or near a roost, say, for re-roofing or timber treatment, the NCC must be consulted for guidance on the timing and method.

Penalties for infringement can be heavy. There is now a

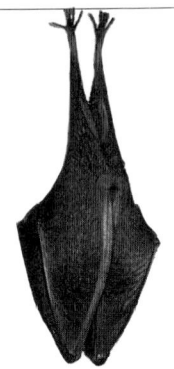

maximum fine of £2,000 and each bat involved can be considered a separate case.

Successful cases have been brought against people harming bats and a recent fine of £1,000, plus costs, against a timber-treatment firm has made such operators very careful.

There is always the danger that people may interfere with bats through ignorance of the law or because they feel that nobody will find out. Increased publicity about the law is essential, not only to householders, but also to timber-treatment firms, builders, surveyors and other trades people likely to work in or near bat roosts. It is also important that Environmental Health Officers and others who might be approached for advice on bats should be well-informed.

In a recent case, a householder, whose wife was frightened of bats, found bats were roosting in his roof-space. He phoned several agencies for advice. It was evening and nobody was well enough informed to contact the NCC or a batworker. The ultimate advice given to the householder was, 'Don't touch them for they are protected and there are heavy fines. The best course is to block up all the holes in your house!'

Not unreasonably, the man followed the advice, waiting until the bats flew out at dusk and then sealing the holes. Unfortunately, it was July and this was a breeding roost. In a short time, the female bats were flying agitatedly around trying to get back to feed their young.

We were called in the following day by the NCC. We explained to the householder that he must unblock the holes or the babies would die, indeed, many of them could have been dead already for it was a very hot day. He was a kindly man and wished the bats no harm, having been merely misled by the wrong advice.

Fortunately, the females returned that evening, but there was no way in which we could find out how many of them found their babies dead.

This is a typical example of how ignorance of the law and incorrect advice, however well-meant, can be disastrous. It emphasises this need for more publicity and education. Needless to say, the agency concerned was quickly advised on how to handle future bat enquiries.

Apart from flagrant breaches, the Act is not intended to be punitive, but rather educational. Successful prosecutions do not restore dead bats, but the publicity of such cases does increase public awareness of the threats to bats and the wide protection which they now have.

It is to be hoped that people will appreciate that there are very sound reasons why bats are now the most highly protected animals in Britain.

9 Working with bats

The Wildlife and Countryside Act, 1981, brought the plight of the bat sharply into focus. The result has been an increasing number of people becoming interested in bats and wanting to work actively for their conservation.

Bat Groups have been formed in nearly every county in Britain. The groups consist mainly of amateurs who have a love for wildlife in general and are fascinated by bats in particular.

Fortunately, because so little is known of the bat's secrets, there is a great deal that inexperienced amateurs of all ages can do to increase our knowledge. Even young children can do valuable work by taking part in our national surveys of bat roosts.

Closer involvement with bats requires a licence. This is normally only issued after specialised training in handling techniques, bat biology and life-style, and instruction in interpreting the law relating to bats.

There are several grades of licence. The first is the basic bat-roost visitor's licence. This allows the holder to visit roosts in houses, to catch occasional bats by hand or hand-net for identification or to show to householders before being released. It allows the examination of bat-boxes, but does not permit visits to hibernation roosts.

The bat survey and research licence covers catching bats by techniques requiring more skill. Special additional training is required for this licence.

The ringing and marking licence is rarely granted and must be for a definite and worthwhile purpose. Again, it requires special training.

Finally, there is the trainer's licence. This is a licence granted to a small number of batworkers, licensing them to train others up to licence-holding standard.

When the Wildlife and Countryside Act, 1981, became law, it prevented unlicensed people, such as Environmental Health Officers, from handling cases of enquiry or complaint about bats. All such cases had to be referred to the Nature Conservancy Council. It soon became clear that the NCC would be quite unable to handle the great number of cases which were occurring. The use of licensed batworkers was an obvious answer to the problem.

The result was that batworkers found themselves deeply involved in important practical work in bat conservation. In the summer they were particularly busy and what had started as a casual interest for some, now became a demanding and absorbing hobby.

Fortunately, the equipment needed for batworkers is simple and inexpensive. A helmet is necessary to protect the head, particularly in caves and mines. Overalls are sensible. A good torch or headlamp is vital, always with spare battery and bulb. In fact, we always carry both hand-torch and headlamp. A suitable ladder or folding steps is often necessary, as they are not always available, even in houses. Because many attics are insulated with glass-fibre and we find it unpleasant, we use industrial masks in such places.

 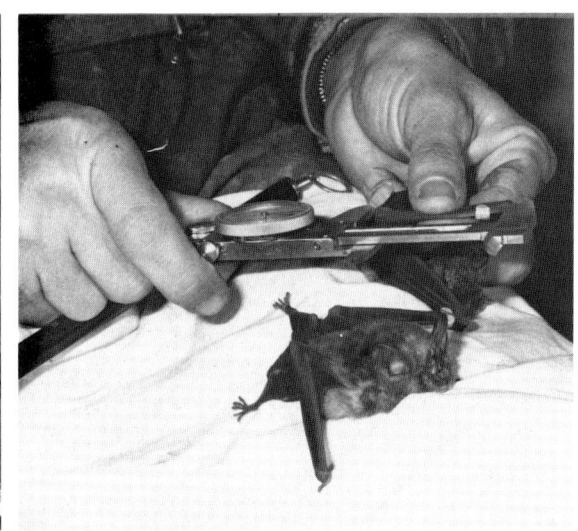

Dr. Roger Ransome, Greater Horseshoe expert, weighs a bat for record purposes.

Using a pair of calipers to measure a bat's forearm. Another Greater Horseshoe waits its turn.

Bat detectors are useful and interesting, but not essential. They are fairly expensive, but those with talents in electronics can make their own. Calipers for taking forearm measurements and a balance for weighing bats are only necessary if more detailed work is being performed.

The nature of bat casework varies tremendously. Sometimes it requires no more than reassuring a householder that bats are harmless. Occasionally a householder wants a bat caught and its species identified, often because they are curious about their resident bats.

Other cases may call for a great deal of ingenuity in overcoming the practical problems. People may need urgent roof repairs or timber-treatment and are anxious not to break the law. Vicars protest about the droppings in their church. People complain about the excited twittering as bats prepare to leave the roost in the evening. Others fear that bats will breed like mice or might even bite the children!

Batworkers must be prepared to climb into attics, which is the site of most casework roosts. Not everyone need take on the more precarious tasks, but someone has to deal with the cases in trees, belfries, caves and mines, many of them uncomfortable and dirty places.

Horseshoes favour the roofs of limestone caves. John explores likely spots in Gwent.

Working with bats means inevitable late nights, particularly in mid-summer, and needs considerable patience.

Each case is different and carries its own challenge and excitement. Will it be a rare species? Will it be a really tough problem and, if so, can the bats be saved? Can the reluctant

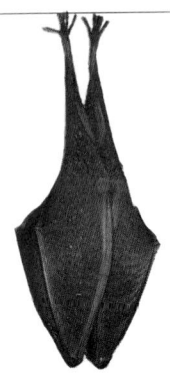

householder be won over to the bat's cause? Surprisingly, the answer is that usually they can, but it takes patience, tact and persuasive skills.

There was the old inn where baby bats were falling through the ceilings on to beds with the results that guests were leaving hurriedly. Blocking up all holes with foam rubber saved the proprietor a lot of money and the bats were allowed to stay.

There was the lady who phoned to say she had bats and what should she feed them on!

One householder said that the bats had filled his attic with straw and twigs. It took quite a lot of persuasion to convince him that it was starlings that were to blame and that bats made no nests.

Quite often bat-haters slowly turn into bat-lovers and even join their local Bat Group. One lady, who was adamant that the bats must be removed, listened to our explanation of the reasons for bats needing roosts in houses. At the end, we asked what she wanted us to do about the bats, to which she fiercely replied, 'Nobody is going to touch *my* bats!'

A sick Long-eared Bat, poisoned by Lindane used for treating woodworm.

One of the most difficult tasks facing batworkers is caring for ailing or injured bats. Not everyone has the aptitude for this aspect of bat conservation. It is time-consuming, testing of patience and all too often heart-breaking. However, gaining the trust of a wild creature, having it feed from your hand, even come when you call it, are truly satisfying and rewarding experiences. There is a special delight in being able to release a bat back into the wild. However, if a bat has been in care for some time, it is unlikely that it can be safely released, in which case they usually become rather pampered pets for the rest of their lives.

Few vets know anything about bats and it is up to batworkers either to learn bat nursing skills or to encourage a friendly local vet to develop them. Fortunately, our vet, Jean, treats our bats with the same gentle concern she has for all animals.

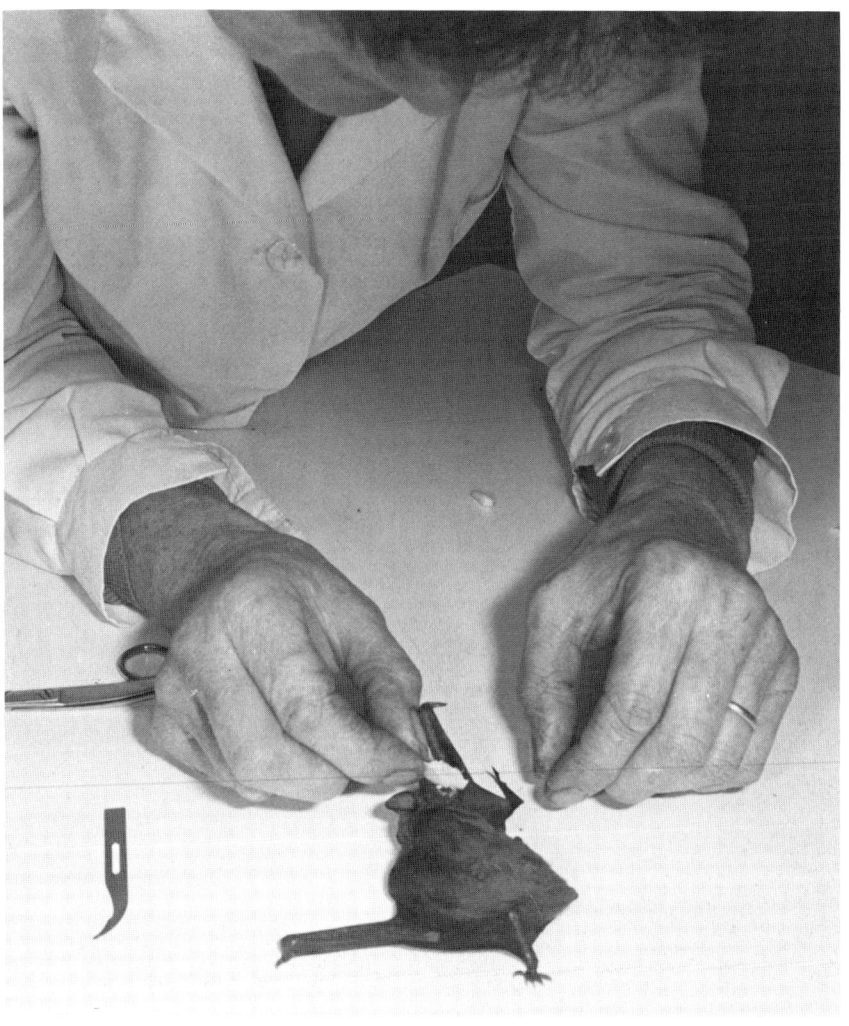

Some bat injuries require professional veterinary care. Jean Morris, our vet, prepares a patient for surgery.

Torn membranes heal quickly, but a tear through the edge requires stitching. Other small mammals can have broken limbs set with splints, but the bat's membranes get in the way and prevent this being done effectively.

Often broken bones are poking through the flesh or will do so if the bat is handled carelessly. Although a number of ingenious methods have been used to splint broken arms, they have met with limited success. It appears that veterinary pinning is by far the best solution.

Any rescued bat should be given water to drink immediately, as it may well be short of liquids. We use a small plastic dropper and find that bats will normally start drinking with no difficulty.

Feeding bats is a problem and, although we know batworkers who sometimes use tinned pet food, hard-boiled eggs, bananas and other strange and unnatural diets, we rely almost entirely on mealworms. These are obtained from a good pet shop, but we also breed our own, only buying in bulk when we have a lot of bats or some of the larger species.

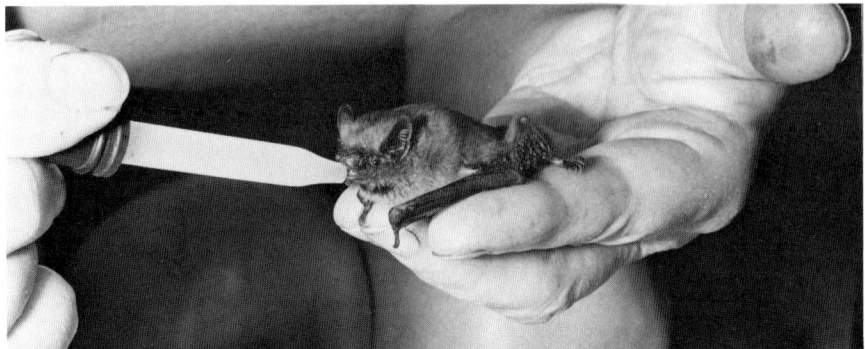

Older bats will take liquids readily from a dropper.

Bats often start to feed immediately they are offered a mealworm. Other bats may be very low and refuse to eat, but they must be coaxed and even forced if they are to survive. It may sound rather gruesome, but we cut the head off a mealworm and offer the bat the body, moistening its lips with the juices. If it continues to refuse, we gently but firmly pack a piece of mealworm into its mouth. Mealworms turn into beetles and the larger bats enjoy these.

Invalid bats must be weighed every few days to make sure they are maintaining their weight.

A diet of mealworms is incomplete and, after a few weeks, an

Mealworms are the staple diet of bats in care, after weaning.

otherwise fit bat may start to decline. We feed them a drop or two of vitamins intended for human babies, usually Abidec, obtained from the chemist.

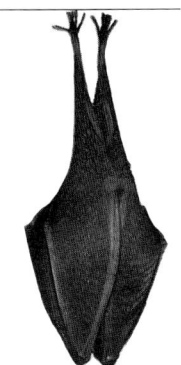

The mealworms themselves need to be well fed. We give them dry oatmeal, bran and wholemeal flour, supplemented with fresh raw cabbage, apple and other vegetables. We also give them ground up high protein fish food.

Bats will usually learn quickly to eat from a dish and drink from a water bowl or dispenser. This is an important step as it saves an enormous amount of time.

Once bats are capable of flying, they should be allowed to do so daily. This is not always possible as the larger bats, such as the Noctule, need plenty of room in which to fly. When bats are released they must be taken back to their own locality. Unfortunately, observations suggest that bats which are nursed for a few weeks probably lose their ability to survive in the wild. The critical decision is whether to let them take their chance or to keep them in captivity.

We give all our bats names, not merely because we are sentimental, but because it makes it easier for us to record and remember them.

Fred, an elderly Pipistrelle, whose finger injuries meant that he would never fly properly again, lived with us for nearly two years. He regularly came with us when we lectured on bats and lent his charms to our statements that bats are delightful little creatures. Fred even came on caravanning holidays with us, for, although you can ask neighbours to look after the cat, a bat is another matter!

Bryn, a Long-eared Bat, was rescued from timbers which had been sprayed with deadly Lindane. He was a feeble little animal, much under weight, with his fur dull and staring. After a great struggle, we managed to get him feeding. He gradually put on weight, his coat shone and he flew round the room with ease.

Bryn's favourite game was to hide behind the curtains and slowly peep out at us. He never seemed to realise that his huge ears gave away his position long before he could see us!

Sadly, the Lindane had done its damage. Suddenly, Bryn went off his food and two days later he was dead.

Willy, a baby Whiskered Bat, fell out of a roost and was found close to death. We guessed he was about 17 or 18 days old, not quite old enough to fly. We gave him cow's milk, slightly diluted. He picked up very quickly and was restored to his mother.

Lloyd, an adult Whiskered Bat, got his name from being found in a local Lloyd's Bank. He was an elegant bat, but very hungry and thirsty, probably having been accidentally shut up for some

Bryn, our Long-eared
Bat, peeping
mischievously round
the curtain in our
cottage.

time. Eventually, Lloyd was released in the garden behind the bank.

One of our most difficult tasks was to cope with Norma and Noreen, a pair of female Noctules sent to us by the RSPCA. Both of them had severe forearm fractures, with the bones protruding. In addition, they were both pregnant.

Noreen would eat well, but Norma had to be forced until she got the idea. Jean, our vet, set the arms, but Noctules are muscular animals and pulled at the splints which had been glued into place. We reset them several times.

Then Norma, the one in poorest health, had a baby. A tiny, blind and hairless little mite, it clung to its mother's fur with its huge feet. If it got separated from her, it yelled with a surprisingly lusty voice.

The arms had healed, but the bones clearly had failed to set. Both bats were eating and drinking well, but Norma had a sunken look between her shoulder-blades which looked ominous and the baby was only progressing slowly. Clearly, something had to be done about those arms.

A few phone calls and Dr. Bob Stebbings of the Institute of Terrestrial Ecology kindly offered to take them to a vet who agreed to pin the broken bones, a highly specialised task.

The two bats and baby were carefully packed and sent off by British Rail, a distance of 200 miles. Bob collected them, kind-heartedly hanging around the station for them until 2 a.m.

Bob took them to Lesley Helliwell, the vet. Sadly, Norma's wing was now infected and she needed anti-biotics. Finally the wing had to be amputated, but she seemed better for it.

Noreen had a stainless-steel pin fitted from wrist to elbow

inside her forearm. She had her baby, but it was a difficult birth and Lesley had to help her. However, both mother and baby were fine afterwards.

In Chapter 4 we gave details of the steps which should be taken to restore young bats to their mothers. Sometimes, however, the mothers fail to pick them up. The possible reasons for this include the baby being put in the wrong place or, if the evening is chilly, the baby gets cold and torpid and fails to emit its 'isolation cries'. To overcome the latter, the baby should be put out immediately before the adults start to emerge and, if it is cold, a well-wrapped hot-water bottle could be placed in the bottom of the box.

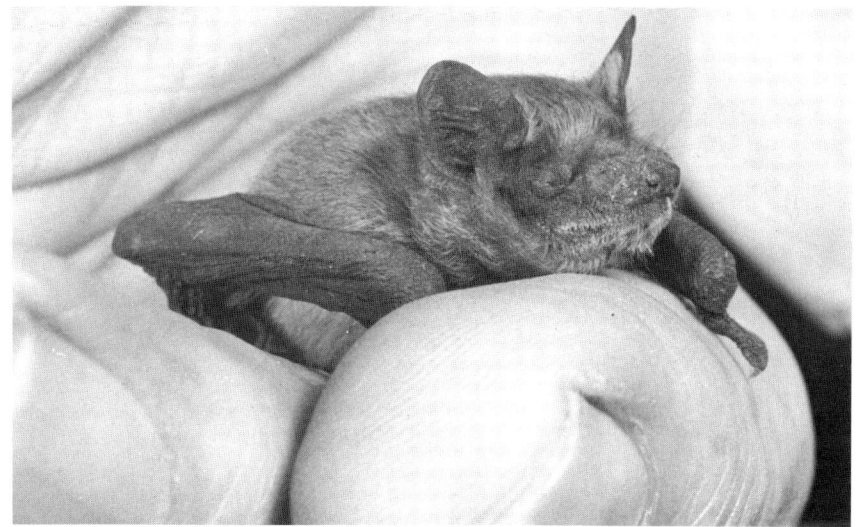

A cold and starving young bat which was eventually saved.

If the mother fails to pick up the baby, then the youngster must be reared by hand.

A naturalist friend of ours has recently attempted to use other lactating pet animals to foster bats, but with little success at this early stage.

At the time of writing this, we are rearing four young bats, with another being delivered any day. They are at a warm temperature of about 30°C, using a small seed-propagator. Feeding can be either with three parts of cow's milk, diluted with one of water, or a patent dried milk for pets, such as Lactol, adding one drop of Abidec vitamins every two or three days. The feed should, of course, be warm.

Young bats have problems with even tiny droppers and the best solution seems to be using a good water-colour paintbrush. Once the bat starts feeding from the tip of the brush, a dropper can be used to drip a gentle flow of milk on to the brush.

We feed about every 1–2 hours. Weighing is essential to check

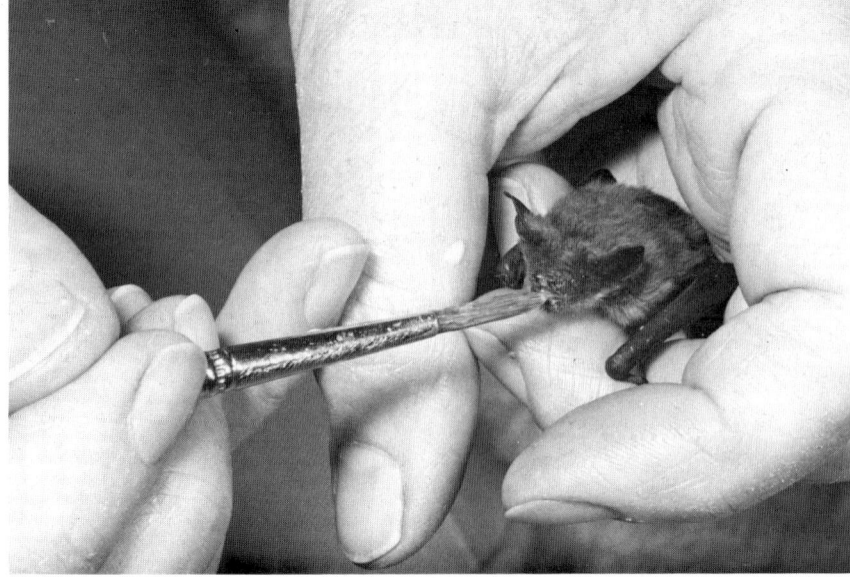

Very young bats are
given a liquid feed
with a paintbrush.

progress. Reducing the temperature at night slows their
metabolism and allows us to get some sleep. We give the last feed
about midnight and the first about 6.30 a.m.

We know two naturalists who put a drip of honey in the feed.
It is unnatural, but we have tried it and must admit that it seems
to encourage reluctant feeders.

The bats should fly at about three weeks. It is fascinating to
watch them trying out their wings. First they stretch out one
wing, together with the leg on the same side, which fully extends
the membrane. Then they try the other wing and, finally, both
wings.

Their first attempt to fly is a hop and flutter of a few inches.
Then they manage a little farther and finally take off to fly
round the room. The first flights are erratic, with a few
collisions, but very quickly they are flying with the superb skill
of an adult.

As soon as a young bat starts to fly, it would normally start
supplementing its diet by catching insects. So, from three weeks,
we start mixing the milk with juices squeezed from mealworms.
As soon as they will take it, they are given small pieces of
mealworm until they can eat a whole one. Normally, they would
be weaned at about five weeks, but artificial feeding is less than
perfect and may have to be continued a little longer. From the
start of weaning, bats should always have access to drinking
water.

Some naturalists carry the baby in a cotton bag round their
necks against their bodies for warmth! This can create a number
of obvious problems and we prefer the propagator.

A team of batworkers
weighing, measuring,
ringing and recording
animals in a
Herefordshire mine.

Finally, playing regularly with captive bats is an important
factor in their wellbeing, both for youngsters and adults.

There is no doubt that for amateurs working with bats to be
most effective, they should join a Bat Group. The sharing of
skills and the pooling of knowledge can help everyone and avoids
duplication of effort.

Members of Bat Groups often organise regional or national
surveys of a specific aspect of bats. They may focus their
attention on a local species of even study one roost in depth. In
this way they can often make very valuable contributions to our
scant knowledge of the bat's secrets.

It must be stressed that any inexperienced person attempting
to aid an ailing or injured bat or to rear an abandoned youngster,
should always seek the advice of the NCC or their local Bat
Group. Not only does this offer the best prospects for the bat,
but it also establishes the individual's credibility if the question
of illegal possession of the animal should arise.

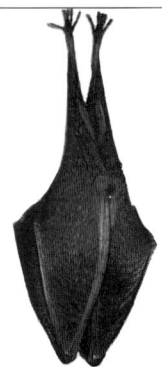

10 Bat-boxes

Although bird-boxes are a common sight in both town and country gardens, very few people think of putting up bat-boxes. Happily, the situation is changing and, although it is most unlikely that they will ever approach the popularity of bird-boxes, there is no doubt that bat-boxes are on the increase.

One of the greatest threats to bats is the loss of their roosting sites, particularly for breeding and hibernation. Conservationists are fighting hard to prevent this loss continuing, but a vast number of roosts have undoubtedly gone for ever. Although the contribution made by bat-boxes will be small, nevertheless it can still be significant. In addition, the very existence of bat-boxes in gardens arouses curiosity and discussion, which can draw attention to the issues surrounding the bat and its battle for survival.

Artificial roosts are not new. In the USA, huge bat-towers were constructed as long ago as 1911 to encourage bats to roost and breed as a means of controlling disease-bearing mosquitoes. It was also hoped that they would produce a large amount of guano and actually show a profit. Unfortunately, the scheme failed.

A great deal of thought and experiment has gone into both the design and the siting of bat-boxes. One of the most significant contributions in this field has been the BBC Nationwide Bat-box Scheme which is an ongoing experiment of Dr. Bob Stebbings. It resulted in the sponsorship of several thousand boxes, which were set up in a variety of British forests.

The boxes were placed at two heights and facing the four points of the compass. This gave valuable information on the roosting preferences of the various species and provided our main guidance for future bat-box schemes.

The box used in the scheme is well-tried and very effective. It is generally known as the standard or conventional box. It is cheap and easy to make. As in most bat-boxes, it is made from rough-sawn timber at least 25 mm thick.

The timber of bat-boxes is never planed or sanded as the roughness of the wood, both inside and out, enables the bat to hang on to the timber when entering or exploring the box.

Boxes should never be painted or treated with preservatives as the smell would discourage bats and some preservatives might even harm them. Without treatment, even soft-wood boxes will last many years.

Bat-boxes on the BBC
Nationwide Bat-box
scheme at Cannock
Chase forest.

New developments in bat-boxes have produced a number of
successes, many of them refinements of the standard box. To
date, we have produced five models, each one, we believe, an
improvement on its predecessor.

The standard box has several shortcomings. The lid often
warps with weathering. This can loosen it, so that it is no longer
weatherproof and light-tight. Warmth generated by the body heat
of a colony can disperse too easily through an ill-fitting lid, which
defeats the purpose of using thick wood to retain heat. The
warped lid could be blown off in high winds or could even be
removed by predators. It is true that fitting catches would go
some way towards overcoming this problem.

Bats generally cling to the underside of the lid, so when it is
removed for examination the bats come with it. This creates
problems for the batworker, who may be hanging on to a high
ladder with one hand and holding a lid with awakening bats
clinging to it in the other. Also, great care is needed to prevent
trapping bats' wings and toes when replacing the lid. We have
seen twenty-six bats in one box and even fifty or more have been
found, clearly quite a handful!

Another weakness of the standard box is its popularity as a nesting box for birds. Ensuring that the entrance slot is no greater than 20 mm will help, but it still allows tree-creepers and blue-tits in. We have had tree-creepers taking over boxes within days of them being sited and rearing a family in them in a matter of weeks.

Unfortunately, blue-tits tend to clutter up the entrance slot with nesting material. In a box in our garden, we found a brood of dead fledglings which had been unable to escape for this reason.

Our latest design appears to overcome some of these problems. This is its first season in use and it is still undergoing tests. However, we are sufficiently confident in its prospects to start installing them extensively in Gwent nature reserves.

We call it the 'Tanglewood Wedge' after the name of our cottage and the fact that it is wedge-shaped. It is front-opening, which enables examination with the minimum of disturbance. The door does not have to be removed, so the batworker has both hands free. Although birds have visited them, none of the Wedges have had nests built in them, for there is no flat floor for easy building.

The shape of the box provides a pocket of warm air at the top and the fact that we nail and glue ensures the minimum leakage of warm air. The box has about the same capacity as the standard box, but the bulk of the space is at the top, where the bats would tend to clump together. The box is easy to make, wind and watertight and has no expensive hinges.

There were fears that the Wedge's inward-sloping front would be too oblique to the sun's rays and might result in a colder box. With this in mind, we ran comparison tests using a number of digital thermometers. The standard box did warm up more quickly, but within thirty minutes the temperature of the Wedge had caught up and passed it. From then on it was warmer all day and remained warm longer after sunset.

One of the strengths of the Wedge, we believe, is that it will be more efficient at retaining heat generated by a colony of bats using the box, making it highly suitable for breeding and possibly hibernation roosts.

We must stress, however, that the standard box has proved itself over many years and, although we have every confidence in the Wedge, it is relatively new.

Only simple rough carpentry with few tools is required for the Wedge. A resin glue must be used, which is odourless when dry. We use Cascamite, which is simple to use and fills gaps left by our less than perfect carpentry. We pre-drill nail-holes undersize to avoid splitting the cheap timber used. The hinges are simply two galvanised clout-nails, normally used for fixing roofing felt.

Although the wood is left rough, we still heavily score the inside of back-board, sides and roof with the point of an old wood-chisel to give the bats a better toe-hold. In addition, we make horizontal saw-cuts on the lower part of the back-board. Probably the saw-cuts are unnecessary, but they might just encourage a half-interested bat. If the wood is purchased ready-planed, then scoring and saw-cuts are essential.

Practically any readily available timber will do and most bat-boxes are made of soft-wood. It is cheaper and usually rougher if bought straight from the sawmill. The thickness of the wood may vary from 25 mm, but it should be thicker rather than thinner. If the thickness is other than 25 mm, then this will alter some of the other dimensions. For this reason, it is wise to make

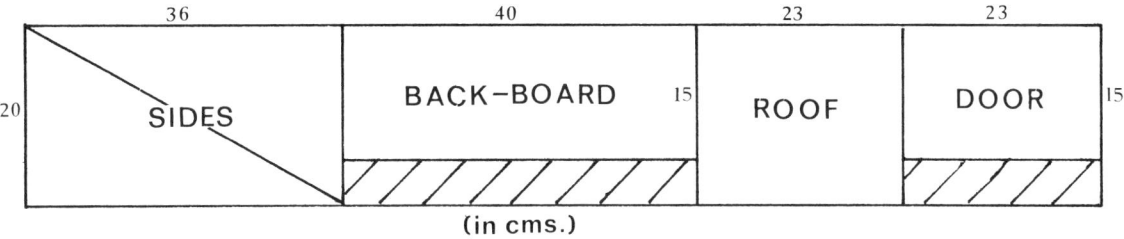

Fig 1 Cutting plan

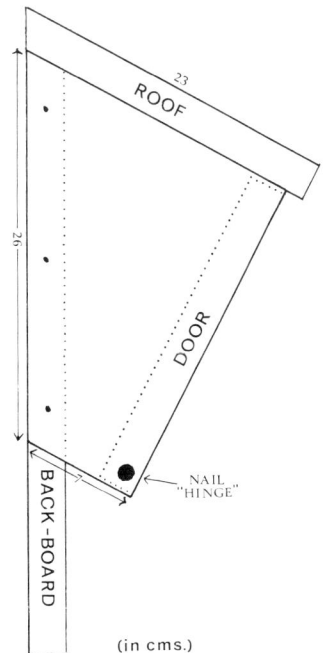

Fig 2 Side view

the first box step by step rather than cutting all pieces at once.

The Wedge is cut from a plank 20 cm wide. The sides are made first. They are made from a piece 36 × 20 cm, which is then cut diagonally from corner to corner. Triangular pieces are cut off the sides as in Fig. 3. The position of the cuts controls the size of the entrance slot. To give an entrance of 20 mm when using 25 mm timber, the cut should be 7 cm long and 26 cm from the top of the side, as shown. It is simple to enlarge the entrance by chamfering a little off the inside edge of the door.

The back-board is 40 × 15 cm. One edge on both the back-board and the roof require bevelling. This can be done in one operation if a circular or jig-saw with tilting facility is available. In this case, the back-board and roof can be cut from one piece 63 × 20 cm, with the saw tilted to approximately 62° and used to cut off a piece 23 × 20 cm to form the roof. This method

Fig. 3.
Side of bat-box showing the position of cut.

Fig. 4.
Side with door-stop nailed in place.

Fig. 5.
Side and back-board glued and nailed.

gives both pieces the correct bevel. Otherwise bevels must be planed, using the top of the side as a guide to the correct bevel. If desired, the roof can be made longer to give a greater overhang.

The back-board should then be sawn to reduce its width to 15 cm.

The side door-stops are now fitted. These are 10–12 mm square and 20 cm long. Two are required. They are nailed on to the sides, as in Fig. 4. They should be flush with the top edge and set back from the front edge of the sides by 25 mm, or by the thickness of the wood if this is other than 25 mm.

The sides are nailed and glued on to the back-board, as in Fig. 5, followed by nailing and gluing the roof, Fig. 6. Check for gaps and run glue in to seal them, if necessary. For large gaps, a mixture of glue and fine sawdust is preferable.

The top door-stop must be tailor-made to fit, see Fig. 7.

Carefully mark the sides for the door pivot points at 12.5 mm from the bottom and 12.5 mm from the front edge. Drill the holes slightly smaller than the clout nails which will form the hinges. It is important that the holes should be in line with each other.

The door is now cut to 23 × 15 cm. The long edges of the door are planed to give 1–2 mm clearance on each side of the door when in position. Pieces of cardboard are inserted at the sides and top to maintain 1–2 mm clearance. Holding the door firmly closed with a clamp or by hand, holes are drilled through the existing pivot-holes into the edge of the door. The clout nails

Fig. 6 (left). Side, backboard and roof glued and nailed.

Fig. 7 (right). The top door-stop must be tailor-made to fit.

Fig. 8.
Door clamped shut
and cardboard
distance pieces in
position.

are then hammered home. Another hole is drilled which will be
an easy fit for a third clout nail. This hole is near the top of one
side 12.5 mm back from the edge and is drilled through the side
and into the edge of the door. This clout nail keeps the door
closed. A small screw is screwed half home into the front of the
door near the top to act as a knob for opening the door. The
cardboard distance pieces are then removed.

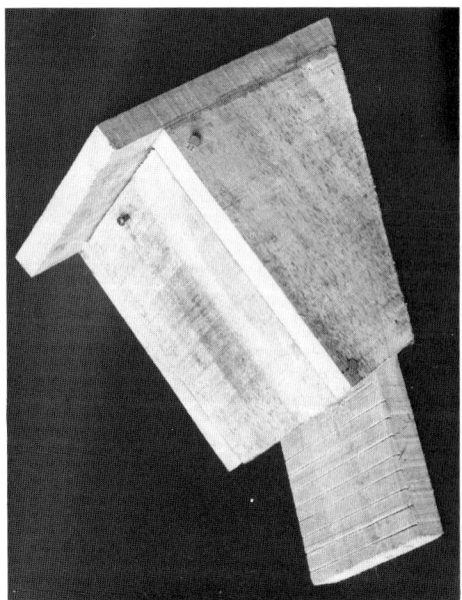

Fig. 9 (right).
Completed box with
door closed.

Fig. 10 (far right).
Completed box with
door open.

Check that the door pivots correctly and that the entrance slot is within the limits of 15–20 mm.

For those wishing to build the standard box, we highly recommend an excellent booklet entitled 'Bat Boxes – their History, Function and Construction' by Bob Stebbings and Sheila Walsh. In addition, it contains a great deal of interesting and valuable information about bat-boxes and their siting. It can be obtained free by sending an SAE 22 × 15 cm to The Bat Conservation Officer, FFPS, c/o Zoological Society of London, Regent's Park, London, NW1 4RY.

The common practice for attaching bat-boxes to trees has been nailing. However, if the trees are destined for the sawmill then copper or aluminium nails must be used to avoid damaging the saw. The growth of trees sometimes breaks boxes which are nailed on. Other methods are used and some of these are described in the bat-box booklet.

We are now using medium-weight fencing wire straps which prove very satisfactory.

We put a length of wire round the tree and twist the ends together, leaving long ends for future annual adjustment. Another length is put on about 35 cm lower down the tree. We hammer a 25 mm staple into each corner of the back of the box, partially pre-drilling the holes first. A piece of wire about 35 cm long is put through the two top staples and twisted onto the top wire

Two bat-boxes wired to a tree and ready for occupation.

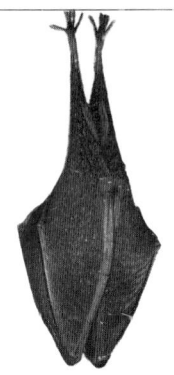

strap. A similar piece is put through the two lower staples and attached to the lower strap.

The straps could be threaded directly through the staples, but as we put up three boxes at a time, the weight would be difficult to handle. Also, with this method, single boxes can be removed and replaced if necessary.

The siting of boxes is critical for the success of the scheme. Ideally, they should be in an area which is short of natural roosts, for example coniferous plantations. However, the sites should be rich in feeding areas used by bats. Needless to say, the permission of landowners should always be sought before setting up boxes.

We follow the advice of Bob Stebbings and place our boxes facing south-east and south-west, with an additional box facing north to offer a cool alternative for very hot weather. The last could be omitted if only a few boxes are being set up.

We place them as high up the tree as possible, but still giving reasonable access for inspection. Bats prefer a clear flight to the boxes and so we remove as much of branches and undergrowth as we can for a metre or two above and under the box. The tree should be clear of neighbouring trees and should also receive some direct sunshine.

Boxes must be examined regularly, probably once a month from May until October. Even if bats are not present, droppings should be looked for. One disadvantage of the Wedge is that droppings tend to fall out. However, a few usually adhere to the fibres of the wood or one could fix a small strip on the lower edge of the back-board to catch the droppings.

The law relating to bat-boxes is a little tricky. Technically speaking, a box does not become a roost until bats occupy it, so it is not unreasonable to presume that boxes could be examined until that happy day when bats are found in residence. From then on the box can be observed, but not examined without a licence. With such a licence, boxes can be opened, examined, bats handled and identified, which make the whole exercise much more interesting and worthwhile.

It is important to keep records of the bat-boxes and their occupation. The Institute of Terrestrial Ecology is always grateful for accurately kept information. To have real value, records should be kept over a number of years.

People often want to encourage bats into their houses. It is important to check first that the house timbers have never been treated with Lindane. Access can be simply provided by boring 20 mm holes in soffits or barge-boards, but there is no other way of encouraging bats except to ensure that the garden is rich in night-flying insects by growing suitable plants.

In addition to bat-box schemes, there are many projects to

The grilling of caves and mines to reduce interference to bats is very valuable for bat conservation. The World Wildlife Fund supported the construction of this grill. The mine is both a breeding and hibernation roost for Lesser Horseshoe Bats.

provide or adapt alternative roosts for bats. Whipsnade Zoo, for example, is building an artificial cave which they hope will attract wild bats.

Bat Groups are often involved in quite ambitious schemes, such as modifying disused tunnels, cellars and mines to make them more attractive to bats.

Caves are often fitted with heavy grills to prevent unauthorised access. Such grills are expensive and their installation and other bat-conservation schemes have been supported by the NCC, the World Wildlife Fund, the Mammal Society, the Fauna and Flora Preservation Society and other wildlife organisations.

Finally, anyone contemplating an ambitious bat-box scheme or wishing to attract bats to their house, should contact the NCC or their county Bat Group for expert advice before doing so.

11 The future of bats

Records show that bats in Britain have been diminishing in numbers over many years. Occasionally, they seem to have a slightly successful year when good weather and their instincts for survival overcome all the hazards that man has created for them. Sadly, this encouraging episode never lasts, for a harsh winter and a cold, wet spring bring their numbers tumbling down again.

The new Wildlife and Countryside Act, which was better late than never, must be of some help. The increase in interest in bats and the new wave of enthusiasm for their conservation are important steps forward. Yet, despite these encouraging signs, bats have by no means won their fight for survival and there is no indication that the trend has reversed.

Education, particularly of young people, is vital for bats. Here, Dr. Bob Stebbings outlines some finer points of a Lesser Horseshoe Bat.

Too many people still cling stubbornly to the folklore of the past, believing bats to be evil or at least pests. Disturbance continues in caves and other roosts. Most farmers and gardeners use harmful insecticides extensively. Woodland and hedgerows continue to disappear at an alarming rate, never to be replaced.

The simple truth is that the greatest enemy of this gentle and harmless animal is man and the reasons are those of ignorance, prejudice and selfishness.

The balance could be tipped in the bat's favour, but it needs a great number of caring people. Particularly it needs young people. Young people who are relatively free from the prejudices of superstition and folklore and who are prepared to think for themselves about the justice of the bat's cause.

If more people join their County Trusts for Nature Conservation, the Mammal Society, the Fauna and Flora Preservation Society, or similar organisations throughout the world, and if more support their local Bat Groups, then bats could have a future.

Our personal interest in bats began with curiosity and fascination at their intriguing life-style. It developed when we appreciated the total injustice of the way in which they were treated and the desperate need for voices raised to support their cause. Finally, on close acquaintance, we discovered that bats were warm, intelligent and truly endearing little animals and we have respected and loved them ever since.

Bats flew freely in the air millions of years before man walked the earth. It would be a shameful thing if, due to man's intolerance, these truly delightful little creatures were now to disappear for ever.

Useful addresses

Dr. Bob Stebbings,
Institute for Terrestrial Ecology,
Monkswood Experimental Station,
Abbots Ripton, Huntingdon, PE17 2LS.
(Technical information and advice on bats)

The Mammal Society,
Burlington House, Piccadilly,
London, W1V 0LQ.

The Fauna & Flora Preservation Society,
c/o Zoological Society of London,
Regents Park, London, NW1 4RY.
(Information on County Bat Groups)

World Wildlife Fund,
11–13, Ockford Rd., Godalming,
Surrey, GU7 1QU.

Nature Conservancy Council,
Northminster House,
Peterborough, PE1 1UA.
(Bat licences)

Royal Society for Nature Conservation,
The Green, Nettlesham,
Lincoln, LN2 2NR.
(Information on County Trusts for Nature Conservation to which many Bat Groups are affiliated)

QMC Instruments Ltd.,
229 Mile End Road, London E1 4AA.
(Bat Detectors)

Index